DREAMS

EXPLORING THE SECRETS
OF YOUR SOUL

Other Books in the Sacred Psychology Series
by Marilyn C. Barrick, Ph.D.

Sacred Psychology of Love:
The Quest for Relationships That Unite Heart and Soul

Sacred Psychology of Change:
Life as a Voyage of Transformation

Emotions:
Transforming Anger, Fear and Pain

DREAMS

EXPLORING THE SECRETS
OF YOUR SOUL

Marilyn C. Barrick, Ph.D.

SUMMIT UNIVERSITY ☾ PRESS

We gratefully acknowledge the following publishers for permission to reprint excerpts from their copyrighted material: From *Heart,* copyright © 1975 by Agni Yoga Society. From *Snow Lion,* Summer 1998 Newsletter and Catalog Supplement, copyright © 1998 by Snow Lion Publications. From *Shambhala: In Search of the New Era,* by Nicholas Roerich, published by Inner Traditions International, Rochester, Vermont; revised edition copyright © 1990 by the Nicholas Roerich Museum.

DREAMS: *Exploring the Secrets of Your Soul*
by Marilyn C. Barrick, Ph.D.

Visit Dr. Barrick's web site at www.spiritualpsychology.com.

Cover painting: Roxanne Duke

Library of Congress Control Number: 2001087042
ISBN: 0-922729-63-8

SUMMIT UNIVERSITY 🌰 PRESS

I dedicate this book to the soul and
Higher Self of those who would explore their
dreams—dramas that outplay their soul's
adventures on Earth and lessons that would
propel the soul toward oneness with Spirit.

Whether a reflection of daily doings,
a sublime experience of higher levels of
consciousness, or a dip into depths of pain yet
to be resolved, dreams are a remarkable
pathway to unveiling the secrets of your soul.

May your dreams and visions move
you onward to a deeper reflection upon the
mysteries of life and a commitment to the
upward journey of your soul through time
and space and beyond.

Contents

Acknowledgments

I offer this book with the gratitude of my heart and soul to Jesus Christ, Gautama Buddha, El Morya, Kuthumi, Djwal Kul and all the adepts of East and West who have followed their dreams to the starry heights of ascension's light. I send my love and appreciation to my mentors Mark and Elizabeth Prophet, who have loved, blessed and taught me through their dedication, example and delivery of the teachings of the ascended masters.

I gratefully acknowledge the time and expertise of the following individuals, without whose professional and personal assistance this book would not have come to fruition: Karen Gordon for her skillful and creative editing and assistance; Carla McAuley for her valuable edits and ideas; Lynn Wilbert for her expertise in designing and formatting; Roxanne Duke for her beautiful artwork on the cover; Nigel Yorwerth, Patricia Spadaro, Lois Drake and Karen Drye for their helpful input; Norman Millman, Annice Booth and the entire publishing team for their support; and all of my clients, whose dream work has been foundational to the writing of this book. A special thank-you to my friends and family, who have encouraged and supported me every step of the way.

Prologue

The dream is the theater where the dreamer
is at once scene, actor, prompter, stage manager,
author, audience, and critic.

—CARL GUSTAV JUNG
General Aspects of Dream Psychology

Dreams have always been personally meaningful to me. Throughout my life, they have guided and stirred me to explore the inner mysteries of soul and spirit. Their metaphorical messages have revealed depths of my being that I might not have understood in any other way.

My work as a psychotherapist is in transpersonal psychology, meaning the study of human experience that goes beyond the individual's persona, personality or ego. It is an emerging "fourth force" in psychotherapeutic theory, the other three being behaviorism, psychoanalytic theory and humanistic psychology.[1]

The emergence of transpersonal psychology came about because in the 1960s and 1970s clients were reporting experiences that traditional theory did not address or explain to our satisfaction. What was happening to the human psyche when young people were getting "high" or freaked out on psychedelics? How was a therapist to differentiate between a normal person's meditative and mystical experiences and a psychotic's hallucinations and delusions?

Researchers and clinicians alike searched for answers. Emerging evidence came from three main streams: laboratory studies on biofeedback, altered states of consciousness and meditation; therapists' case studies of clients' mystical dreams and meditative work; and anecdotal reports of people's "natural high" experiences.

As transpersonal psychology quickly grew, therapists and researchers developed a new perspective and a new language to explain their findings. We began to hear about paranormal phenomena, transformational experiences and cosmic awareness. Spirituality and the search for the sacred entered the popular consciousness as acceptable life paths.

My work in transpersonal therapy is primarily with people who have been seeking the high road in their lives but have detoured and found themselves stuck somewhere on the low road. They may be uncertain about their direction and confused by their conflicting emotions. Their dream characters and circumstances dramatically portray the ways in which they are stuck and what it will take to free them and get them back on the upward trek.

Dreams can be a map for the soul's journey, unlocking hidden secrets and opening new vistas. I'll tell you one of my own childhood dreams that makes the point.

This was a recurring dream I used to have as a youngster. At that particular time, life seemed scary and confusing to me and I would wake up absolutely nauseated from the following scenario. In my dream there were two huge wire circles that were bigger than the earth, and I had to put the bigger one inside of the smaller one without bending them. The bigger one was dull colored and the smaller one was bright gold.

As a child I didn't understand the message, I just got nauseated. But as I looked back on the dream as an adult, I realized my soul was expressing my absolute frustration with trying to do the impossible. In the dream, I was not only the child trying to do an impossible task, I was also the two circular wires that were bigger than the earth.

What did the wire circles represent? I believe the golden one represented my hopes and dreams, which were going around in circles and not coming true. And the larger, dull-colored one represented my problems, which seemed totally overwhelming and bigger than life to me. My problems were bigger than my hopes and dreams and I couldn't overcome them until I shrank them. (Many dream images carry a message with this kind of dual meaning.)

When I began my work as a transformational therapist, I realized that the solution to my childhood dream was spiritual alchemy and self-transcendence. I could indeed shrink the larger circular wire of my problems and expand the golden circle of my hopes and dreams. Now I could stop running in circles. As I accelerated in spiritual awareness, I would be changing my perspective on seemingly unsolvable situations and realizing my higher vision.

With a sense of excitement and inner joy, I realized the transformational opportunity and I have pursued that journey ever since. My childhood dream has been an inner polestar, always guiding me onward and upward.

I have learned that in the world of dreams our soul becomes a great dramatist with a definite statement to make. As the ego sleeps, the soul, in concert with the Higher Self, uses the sensory impressions of the day to stage an inner message. Our nightly dramas reveal the unique dimensions and inner reflections of our soul. They convey a metaphorical message to the ego, the outer self. The message is a call to action.

Our mystical dreams reveal our divine potential—who we already are in our Maker's eyes, the being we may choose to become. Positive dreams reveal our soul's upward growth and development. Seemingly mundane dreams, cloaked in the sensory impressions of the day, have inner messages about our soul's journey. Even our worst nightmares reveal inner parts of ourselves that are crying out to be healed—traumas, conflicts and hurtful habits that stubbornly plague us from subconscious levels.

The dream message can guide us on an inner healing journey. When the going gets tough, the dream points out old baggage to discard. To our joy and amazement, under the baggage we discover hidden gold.

I have written *Dreams: Exploring the Secrets of Your Soul* for kindred spirits looking for keys to self-transcendence. I hope to ignite an excitement about discovering your magical inner being. I hope to stir you to explore the mysteries inherent in your dreams—to dig into hidden nooks and crannies and toss old baggage, to claim the gold of enlightened understanding and to take wing into higher consciousness.

As you pursue the heights and depths of your own mystical nature, I believe that you, too, will delight in exploring the precious, hidden secrets of your soul. May your journey through dreamland be an illumining and enriching adventure.

Introduction

I will pour out my spirit upon all flesh;
and your sons and your daughters shall prophesy,
your old men shall dream dreams,
your young men shall see visions.

—JOEL 2:28

In my practice as a transformational therapist and as a serious student of the world's mystical truths, I have confirmed for myself that life is a sacred adventure of the soul. Our souls have inner yearnings and mystical secrets ready for our discovery when we pay attention to our lives and to our dreams.

Psychology in its essence is the study of the soul—my soul, your soul. We begin to understand the more obvious nature of our soul when we probe our motivations, thoughts, reactions and behaviors. When we pursue the understanding of our nightly journeys, through our dreams, we are exploring our soul's hidden secrets.

The Journey of the Soul

My understanding of the journey of the soul has its roots in the pursuit of *gnosis,* a Greek term for inner knowing. Raised in a traditional Christian setting, I developed an early sense of inner knowing from my prayers, reading of scripture and communion with Jesus. My soul awareness was also nourished by music, nature and occasional mystical dreams and visions of the heaven world.

As an adult, I meditated and kept track of my inner visions and spiritual dreams. I felt drawn to the mystical aspects of spirituality. My inner nature resonated with the mysteries of the Kabbalah, the Essenes, the Christian mystics and the mystical threads of Buddhism, Hinduism, Taoism and Sufism. I explored esoteric teachings as well—Theosophy, Rosicrucianism, the I AM Activity, the Bridge to Freedom and The Summit Lighthouse.

My own experiences and those of my clients have taught me that we can travel the high road of spiritual initiation and attainment. We can choose to be one with the mind of our Creator, to exercise loving compassion toward everyone we meet and to claim the empowerment of our soul's divine heritage. Our dreams and visions become guideposts along the way.

A Reverence for Spirit

I had the opportunity as a child growing up in Arizona to learn about the customs of many American Indian tribes. Even then I understood their profound reverence for the spiritual essence of all life. And I learned that they considered dreams to be among life's most important experiences.

Native American customs fascinated me. As a teenager I became interested in the way many tribes provided a rite of passage for their youth involving dreams and vision quests. Usually these rituals were for the boys, and I remember wishing I could have a special rite of passage.

Although beliefs and practices differed from tribe to tribe, the Native American people had a heritage of being deeply in touch with the sacred. They saw the divine spirit in nature and in animal life. And they sought divine intervention through dreams, visions and rituals.

Elders and healers would periodically isolate themselves from the rest of the tribe to fast, pray and meditate. They were in pursuit of dreams that would bring guidance and new direction. A common understanding was that the dreamer's strong will and concentration would draw the particular kind of guidance he needed. When I realized that many of these early customs and rituals had not survived into modern times, I was saddened.

Although today Native American cultures are highly respected around the world, in the 1940s and 1950s they were not. I remember seeing Navajo women in Arizona sitting on the pavement selling for undervalued return their beautiful wares of jewelry, pottery, leather goods and blankets. The ever-present souvenirs of Indian headdresses, totem poles and tomahawks perpetuated a stereotyped warlike image. Young men from the reservations faced discrimination and difficulty getting good jobs. They sometimes ended up discouraged and expressed their frustration by drinking and driving wildly over the desert.

I remember thinking, how tragic that "civilization" could so divest us of a sense of honor and civility toward this people. How tragic that the young men and women of the tribes were no longer encouraged by the larger culture to stand tall in their natural reverence for nature and the dignity of their soul and spirit.*

---

*The soul, whether housed in a male or female body, is the feminine counterpart of Spirit. Our spirit (lowercased s) is our masculine essence; thus we say the spirit of a person is joyful, lethargic, melancholy, and so forth.

Fortunately, today we see a renewed respect for Native American traditions, especially in the area of alternative spirituality.

The Life Story of Grandfather

As a prelude to our exploration of dreams, I would like to present a glimpse of the life of Grandfather. He was a revered warrior and shaman of the Lipan Apache tribe who spent his entire life seeking to understand and practice the eternal wisdom of Spirit. His soul's journey speaks to us of the high road of spiritual attainment.

Grandfather cultivated an ongoing connectedness to Spirit through an intuitive approach to everyday tasks. He learned respect for the cycles of nature and had a deep reverence for the essence of the sacred in all life.

The life journey of Grandfather was written by Tom Brown, Jr., a noted wilderness survival trainer.[1] He tells us that Grandfather lived a nomadic existence and trekked through forests, deserts and mountains all over North and South America. In his lifetime Grandfather walked thousands of miles, searching for and communing with his Creator. He walked alone, except when called to teach, to pass on what he had learned.

Following the way of ancient seekers throughout the ages, Grandfather prayed and communed in solitude and obeyed the inner guidance of the Great Spirit. He experienced life-saving lessons from the spirit of God in animal life. For example, a lizard came to his rescue and led him to water when he was in the blazing heat of the desert.

In the land of ice and snow he overcame loneliness and

experienced the unity of all life while watching the Northern Lights. There he was, lying in a snow bank, seemingly alone in the icy wilds, when his intuition prompted him to look around. And sitting in another heap of snow, practically next to him, was a ptarmigan (a kind of grouse), equally engrossed in watching the cosmic lights in the sky.

Grandfather respected all life. He loved and served people. He did his part to take care of nature and understood that we are God's caretakers of the earth. He was a practitioner and teacher of eternal truths, and yet as civilization moved on he saw little of what he taught being transferred to the younger generations. Only the few carried on the ancient sacred traditions.

I pay tribute to Tom Brown for passing on his heritage of Grandfather's walk with the Great Spirit. This captivating story awakens us to the eternal mysteries of God and to holy treasures hidden in the wilderness. We, too, can hear the voice of Spirit within when we listen with heart and mind and soul.

Grandfather's dream of passing on his heritage to future generations is not lost. As we seek to preserve the beauty of nature, return to a more sacred way of life and create inner and outer peace, we are keeping Grandfather's quest and vision alive and well.

Rediscovering Our Identity in Spirit

How do we rediscover our identity in Spirit while leading hectic lives that seem to continually accelerate? How can we be as connected as Grandfather was and receive the promptings of our soul and Higher Self?

I would point to a teaching that runs through all the world's spiritual traditions—that such understanding comes through the highest communion of the heart. A precious book, *Heart,* published by the Agni Yoga society, expresses it beautifully:

> In substance, the heart is an organ of higher action and offering; hence each offering is of the nature of the heart.... Each throb of the heart is a smile, a tear, and gold. All of life flows through the heart....
>
> It is not without reason that the Teaching of the Heart is so needed for the life of the future. Otherwise how will you cross the boundaries of the worlds?... The heart is not wholly one's own organ but is granted for highest communion....
>
> A certain hermit emerged from his solitude with a message, saying to each one whom he met, "Thou possessest a heart." When he was asked why he did not speak of mercy, of patience, devotion, love, and other beneficent foundations of life, he answered, "The heart alone must not be forgotten, the rest will come."
>
> Verily, can we turn toward love, if there is nowhere for it to dwell? Or, where will patience dwell if its abode be closed? Thus, in order not to torment oneself with blessings that are inapplicable, it is necessary to build a garden for them, which will be unlocked to the comprehension of the heart.[2]

Many mystics and spiritual teachers direct their students to commune with Spirit through the heart. Elizabeth Clare Prophet says, "Love is the alchemical key." She reminds us that love is the nature of God and the essence of our own Higher

Self. Love is magnetic. It draws us close to the angels; it draws us close to one another. Love as the compassionate heart heals our pain. It is truly the greatest power in the universe. Where is it to be found on Earth but in the secret recesses of the heart?

And so, as aspiring adepts of the heart, hand in hand with our Higher Self, we can pursue a sacred journey. Our dreams and visions along the way become beacons to guide us. Living the mandates of heaven on Earth, we quicken and illumine the questing of our soul and move ever closer to oneness with the Infinite One.

We begin our journey by exploring the mystical roots of dream interpretation and looking at what people through history have said about dreams. We will look at lucid dreaming and Tibetan dream and sleep yoga as a path of spiritual adeptship through dream work.

Throughout the book, I analyze dreams of friends and clients to show how you can discover the symbology of your own dreams. Together, we will pursue the thread of connection between the dramas of daily life, our nightly dreams and the inner journeys of our soul.

As an explorer of your inner territory, you can journey through your own dream world guided by the pages of this book. You can learn to penetrate your dreams and unveil, layer by layer, the secrets of your soul, the fullness of who you are—and who you may become.

CHAPTER ONE

Mystical Roots of
Dream Interpretation

*Though inland far we be,
Our souls have sight
    of that immortal sea
Which brought us hither.*

—WILLIAM WORDSWORTH
*Ode. Intimations of Immortality
from Recollections of Early Childhood*

*S*ince the dawn of civilization, humanity has been fascinated with dreams and dream interpretations. This is understandable because we spend approximately one-third of our life sleeping, and a good bit of that time dreaming.

A sixty-year-old person, for example, will have spent twenty years sleeping and dreaming. It makes perfect sense that our interest would be kindled. Who wouldn't want to peek into that mysterious otherworld and discover what happens to us while our head is resting on our pillow?

To the ancients, dreams were considered sacred, a way of communing with the divine in the world of Spirit. Experiences in the dream world were taken as seriously as events in waking life. Over thousands of years, dreams and the study of dreams have gained, lost and regained credibility as cultures changed. Yet, all of the ups and downs in credibility have not changed the reality that we do dream.

Guidance from the Great Spirit

As we've seen, Native American tribes highly regarded dreams, for many of the elders and wise men of the tribes were mystics and philosophers. The presence and guidance of the Great Spirit through nature, visions and dreams influenced every aspect of tribal life.

Particularly noteworthy in this respect were the Naskapi in Canada. They lived in small family groups that were isolated from one another and from civilization. Consequently, they had to rely almost entirely on individual inner guidance for the counsel they needed in their lives.[1]

The Naskapi believed the dreamer's soul was an inner companion and friend, Mista'peo, meaning "Great Man." Mista'peo was immortal and dwelled in the heart; following his direction was a sacred obligation. The Naskapi believed that each one must determine what is right by consulting the inner companion, Mista'peo.

This concept of an inner guide is very close to what is known esoterically as the "hidden man of the heart," another way of referring to one's Higher Self. Interestingly, the Naskapi depicted Mista'peo as a mandala, a symbolic circular design, which appears in a similar form much earlier in the Hindu culture.

The mandala is a symbol of wholeness and is considered a universal archetype. Its appearance as a Naskapi image is worthy to note because the people were so isolated they essentially had no contact with other civilizations.

Another interesting tie to Hindu culture is the belief in reincarnation by many tribes in North America, including the Eskimo and the Algonquin. Some even named their children for the person they believed the child had been in a previous life. Manly P. Hall, founder of the Philosophical Research Society, reports a legend where a parent gave his infant the wrong name. As the story goes, the baby cried and cried and could not be comforted until the mistake was corrected and the child had the right name.[2]

While the Naskapi relied on inner guidance, other North American tribes sought deities and guardian spirits for divine inspiration and practical direction. For example, Maricopas attributed all success in life to guidance received from these divine beings during out-of-the-body experiences at night. The Iroquois believed dreams were of greater significance than daytime thoughts because the dreamer had been in contact with the guidance and wisdom of the soul. The Papagos received dream teaching in the form of dream songs. They believed positive actions could come through these songs, such as healing for the sick and rain for the crops.

We find similarities between Native Americans and the Polynesian people of the Hawaiian Islands. From ancient times, the native Hawaiians considered dreams highly important communications. Some were messages from ancestral spirits or the deities of the islands, whose advice was an important source of warning as well as a source of protection, healing and guidance for the future.

The native medical experts, *kahunas,* practiced dream incubation (a special ritual of preparing for, experiencing and remembering dreams) in special temples in order to receive divine healing guidance. Hawaiians also practiced dream incubation in their homes and believed that the soul, the *ʻuhane,* could leave the body during sleep and have out-of-the-body experiences. Dreams were the story of the soul's nightly travels.

Dream Animals: A Manifestation of the Self

Along with many other Native American tribes, the Navajo revered the wisdom and guidance in their dreams as coming from dream animals as well as deities and spirits.

Jungian psychology explains that when an animal appears in a dream it is a manifestation of the Self, our higher inner guiding force. Thus, we come to know the Self by investigating our dreams and visions and understanding ourselves at a deeper level.

When we listen to and heed the inner messages from the Self, we mature psychologically and spiritually. The Self is often symbolized as an animal because it represents the divine essence of our instinctive nature and connectedness with our surroundings.

Jungian analyst M.-L. von Franz reported one woman's meditative experience in which the Self appeared as a deer. The deer said to the woman: "I am your child and your mother. They call me the 'connecting animal' because I connect people, animals, and even stones with one another if I enter them. I am your fate or the 'objective I'. When I appear, I redeem you from the meaningless hazards of life. The fire burning inside me burns in the whole of nature. If a man loses it, he becomes egocentric, disoriented, and weak."[3]

With my own clients, I have seen animal symbolism in the dreams of people who are not Native American but respect their ancient ways. For example, I had a client, an older woman, who loved buffalo. She had the following dream:

"I see two black bull buffalo. I step out of my car right next to them. Their heads are lowered as if to attack. I hesitate, and then I walk off with the buffalo following me. I awaken, thinking, 'That's kind of neat!'"

In her associations she saw buffalo as friendly, protective, majestic. She said, "I'm comfortable with them. They symbolize the life of the Native American people, spiritual people who are in tune with right and wrong through nature. I have a great love for animals. I think I must have been an Indian in a previous incarnation." She added, "The scene in my dream reminds me of a picture I have of two buffalo: one is a regular black buffalo, and the other one is all white, which represents the Great Spirit. In my dream, I have my majestic protectors with me." Her dream message is bold and clear.

Ancient Explanations of the Mysteries of Life

During ancient times (and perhaps also today), the origin and journey of the soul were veiled in mystery. Stories about the soul were cloaked in mythology as people tried to understand and explain the mysteries of life. How did the ancients account for the forces the soul met in everyday life and during nightly travels?

Sometimes they simply personified the powerful forces of nature as mother earth, father sun, brother wind or sister moon. At other times, awed and frightened by seemingly supernatural happenings, they referred to these forces as gods and goddesses or angels, spirits, demons and devils. And they wove archetypal stories around them.

Over millennia, people who revered the sacred were receiving prophetic and enlightening messages. Sometimes the messages were delivered by powerful, unseen spiritual beings. Different cultures across the earth have given names to the invisible source of these messages: the Creator, the Great Spirit, the Tao, Brahman, Ein Sof, God, Elohim, Jehovah, Allah.

Sometimes people had dreams or visions of higher beings, whom they revered as angels, *sefirot* or etheric spirits. If the being was without form, it might be described as brilliant light. In some instances the being would reveal a form and give a specific name, as Archangel Gabriel did when he appeared to Mary in the Visitation and to Muhammad to tell him he was to be Allah's messenger. These powerful spiritual experiences, integral to various cultures, were passed down through the years, from generation to generation.

In every age and culture we find some have pushed beyond the barriers of human understanding to search for a higher knowledge. Such spiritual seekers in the ancient world honored their dreams and lived their sense of the sacred.

The mythology of ancient cultures reminds us that the soul's character and life-path originate in the divine. Our soul is cloaked in mystery upon the earth and our higher character and life-path are forged into the heroic through individual attunement, discernment, determination and decision-making.

Ancient teachings suggest that much of our true nature is hidden and only as we mature over a lifetime, or lifetimes, do the energy patterns of our original divine nature fully emerge and crystallize. Thus, although our essential nature is pure energy, each of us has special gifts inherent in the patterns of our soul.

Like our Creator, our consciousness on all levels is profoundly fluid and changing as we move through our sacred adventures in time and space. Our Higher Self (Christ Self, Buddha Self, Krishna Self, as you will) retains the original divine pattern of our unique identity in Spirit.

CHAPTER TWO

Ancient Records and the Scientific View

*I do not know whether I was then
a man dreaming I was a butterfly,
or whether I am now a butterfly
dreaming I am a man.*

—CHUANG-TZU
On Leveling All Things

*I*n preparation for exploring and analyzing your own dreams, it is helpful to understand how people in different cultures and earlier times explored and interpreted their dreams. We can enrich our interpretations by looking at those from ancient cultures where dream guidance was considered essential to success in life.

We know that records of dream interpretation go back at least to 3000 B.C. Archaeologists have discovered clay tablets in Mesopotamia with dream interpretations inscribed on them, most likely by the Sumerians, who dominated Mesopotamia at that time.[1] These tablets describe three major types of dreams: message dreams, prophetic dreams and symbolic dreams.

Message dreams were the dreams of rulers, wise men and court advisors, although ordinary people undoubtedly had their own unrecorded experiences. These dreams that guided nations were passed down through the ages. They often occurred in a temple where a deity would deliver a personal message to the sovereign or his representative following a dream incubation ritual.

Prophetic dreams were considered to be God's way of unveiling an individual's personal destiny. The third type of dream, symbolic dreams, revealed the dreamer's distinctive characteristics and interactions with the gods, the stars, other people or special objects.

Dream Incubation

In ancient times, people went through special preparations and rituals to access divine guidance through their dreams. In Egypt, for example, Serapis was known as the god of dreams, and *serapims* were the dream temples where people went to have dreams induced. A person seeking advice through dreams would visit a temple, make an offering of some kind, and spend the night in the temple in order to be as close as possible to the gods.

Temple dreams were considered messages from the deities. The practice of dream incubation, or temple sleep, was used for a number of specific purposes, including healing, guidance, prophecies about the future, battle plans, special protection and conception of children.

Scholars believe this practice originated in ancient Sumer and Egypt, spread to Babylon and Assyria, and greatly influenced similar practices in Greece and Rome. Egypt, Babylon, Greece and Rome supported thousands of temples devoted to this practice.

Ancient Dream Journals

Egyptian dream books dating back to about 2000 B.C. list many kinds of dreams and how they relate to the future of the dreamer. Extensive literature from the ancient Semitic cultures of Asia Minor and the Tigris and Euphrates valleys verifies the widespread belief that dreams and visions revealed spiritual realities.

Ancient dream records have also been discovered in India and China. Written between 1500 and 1000 B.C., the sacred Vedas of India offered specific interpretations of dream images (e.g., to ride an elephant was lucky, to ride a donkey was unlucky). The Upanishads, written about 1000 B.C., described the dreamer as abiding in an intermediate state between the spiritual and material worlds. In this state the dreamer gained insights and self-illumination.

In the earliest-known reference to dreams in China (the *T'ung Shu*, 1020 B.C.), we learn that the Chinese believed the soul temporarily left the body during dreams to communicate with the dead. Great care was taken not to rouse people while they slept or the soul might be prevented from reuniting with the body.

The ancient Chinese practiced dream incubation and believed dream images held specific meanings. For example, a dream of the sun or moon rising meant prosperity for one's family, while a dream of an orchard bearing much fruit meant many offspring.

An early reference to dreams was reportedly made by Confucius in the fifth century B.C. Near the end of his life he lamented, "I am declining. It has been a long time since I have seen the Duke of Chou in my dreams."[2] The Duke of Chou was Confucius' mentor, who appeared in Confucius' dreams to exhort him to live a virtuous life.

Dreams in Ancient Greece

In ancient Greece, people went through elaborate incubation rituals to gain access to their dreams, which they believed were visits from the gods.

The town of Epidaurus was a major center where people came to appeal to the physician-god Asclepius for divine direction in their healing. The supplicants would spend their days performing healing practices and their nights in a dream temple awaiting a dream that would guide their further treatment or offer a new glimpse of reality.

The ancient Greeks held various viewpoints about dreams. In the ninth century B.C., Homeric poets depicted dreams as revelations from the gods or other supernatural beings. Later on, the Greeks developed the idea that during sleep the soul left the body and communed with the gods, returning with important information. This information could be either symbolic or direct in nature.

In Homer's epic poem the *Illiad,* Zeus sent a dream figure to Agamemnon. The figure was in the form of the wise old Nestor, king of Pylos and wisest of the Greek chiefs in the Trojan War. The dream figure stood over Agamemnon and roused the Greeks to action.

In the *Odyssey,* Athena formed a phantom woman to bring a message to Penelope. The phantom figure entered through a keyhole and brought to Penelope's dreams the reassurance that her son would return to her. On another occasion, Athena disguised herself and came in a dream to Nausicaä, the daughter of the king of the Phaiacians, to prepare her to help

Odysseus on his final leg of the journey home.

The Greeks in this period also talked about "seeing a dream," rather than dreaming, which might have been a precursor to what is known today as lucid dreaming.

Hippocrates (approximately 460–377 B.C.), known as the father of medicine, placed more emphasis on the diagnostic aspect of dreams, although he also believed in prophetic dreams and those that revealed a person's psychology.[3]

Plato (approximately 427–347 B.C.), student of the great philosopher, Socrates, was noted for his rational way of approaching human experience. However, he also talked about the other side of life, including people's dreams and the way they viewed them.

He believed that during sleep one's reasoning ability was suspended, thereby allowing passions and desires to be released with some abandon. He understood that dreams can reveal the dark, instinctual side of people. In the *Republic* (his greatest work), it is clear Plato accepted that the gods communicate with people through dreams and waking visions.

Aristotle (384–322 B.C.), Plato's pupil and the teacher of Alexander the Great, took a completely rational, empirical point of view. He discounted the idea that dreams were communication with the gods. Instead, he regarded them as natural phenomena prompted by bodily sensations and disturbances. He reasoned that during sleep the soul was more sensitive and could pick up bodily sensations not perceived in the awakened state.

In about A.D. 100, Artemidorus wrote his epic five-volume guide to dreams titled *Oneirocritica (The Interpretation of Dreams)*. It is the most complete work of dream interpretation to have survived from the ancient world. Artemidorus urged flexibility in interpreting dreams for the individual dreamer.

Biblical Dreams and Visions

The Bible has many references to dreams and visions. Do you remember the story of Abimelech and Abraham? Abimelech, king of Gerar, took Abraham's wife, Sarah, into his harem thinking she was Abraham's sister.

Genesis records, "But God came to Abimelech in a dream by night, and said to him, Behold, thou art but a dead man, for the woman which thou hast taken; for she is a man's wife." Abimelech protested his innocence, for he had believed Abraham's story about Sarah being his sister. He also told God he had not touched Sarah. God said to Abimelech in his dream, "Yea, I know that thou didst this in the integrity of thy heart; for I also withheld thee from sinning against me: therefore suffered I thee not to touch her."[4]

God went on to tell Abimelech that if he would immediately restore Sarah to Abraham and ask the prophet to pray for him, his life would be spared. Abimelech quickly did as God instructed. Abraham and Sarah, for their part, learned a hard lesson about fear and lies versus being honest and trusting in God's protection.

The Old Testament also gives the account of Joseph, son of Jacob, who was famed for his prophetic dreams and interpretations. First, we read of Joseph's dream about his brothers bowing down to him, which so infuriated his jealous brothers that they sold him into slavery. Next, we have Joseph's dream interpretations while he was in Pharaoh's prison. He accurately prophesied the death of the baker and the restoration of the chief butler to Pharaoh's service. Then we have the story of Joseph solving the riddle of Pharaoh's dream, in which seven fat cows were devoured by seven lean ones and the seven full ears of corn were devoured by seven thin ones. He interpreted the dream as foretelling seven good years of plenty followed by seven years of famine.

Heeding the dream interpretation, Pharaoh rewarded Joseph handsomely by making him governor of all of Egypt, second in rank only to Pharaoh. Joseph stored extra food during the seven years of plenty. This not only fed the people of Egypt but also fulfilled the prophecy of his earlier dream, for his brothers "bowed down to him" when they came to beg food during the seven years of famine.[5]

In the New Testament we also find respect for dreams as messages from God. The Book of Matthew records the dream of the Magi: "And being warned of God in a dream that they should not return to Herod, they departed into their own country another way."

Matthew also records that the angel of the Lord appeared in Joseph's dream to give him a major warning: "Arise, and take the young child and his mother, and flee into Egypt, and be thou there until I bring thee word: for Herod will seek the young child to destroy him."[6]

What would have happened if they had ignored their dream messages—if the Magi had not "departed another way" or if Joseph, Mary and Jesus had not immediately fled to Egypt? We don't know, of course, but we see that the heavenly hosts were concerned enough to speak directly to them.

Matthew records another attempt at divine intervention, this time through a dream given to Pilate's wife during the trial of Jesus: "When he [Pilate] was set down on the judgment seat, his wife sent unto him, saying, Have thou nothing to do with that just man: for I have suffered many things this day in a dream because of him."[7]

Pilate ignored the dream warning and added insult to injury by placing the responsibility for the crucifixion of Jesus on the people. He "washed his hands" of the entire matter. Such a choice is possible in all divine communication because the Creator has granted his children free will. Divine guidance is given, and the individual receiving it can accept or reject it. Thus, by choice, we move closer to or farther away from divine purpose through our exercise of free will.

Church Fathers on Dreams: From God or Demons?

The early Christian church fathers often placed high value on dreams and dream interpretations. For example, third-century Tertullian wrote that some dreams were gifts from God. He believed dreams could be interpreted on various levels and resulted from any one of four possibilities: either sent by God, caused by demons, created by the soul itself or generated by an unconscious ecstatic state.

He believed people were not accountable for their dream feelings and actions. Author Morton Kelsey comments on Tertullian's position: "Like Plato, Tertullian saw dreaming as akin to madness, a madness in which the soul...is overwhelmed by something other than sense experience. This is closely related to the idea...that psychosis is the living out of one's dream life without orientation to the physical world. We might translate Tertullian's meaning into modern terms by saying that in sleep the unconscious makes its autonomous impression on the...consciousness in the form of the dream."[8]

Origen of Alexandria, also a third-century church father, believed that God revealed himself through dreams, waking visions and divine inspirations. These were all ways in which God gave people symbolic knowledge of the spiritual world. Origen pointed out that God had favored many saints with these divine happenings and that people had been converted from their pagan ways by visions and dreams. He did, however, caution that one must distinguish between dreams from God and those originating from evil spirits.[9]

In the fourth and fifth centuries, the church's attitude toward dreams began to change. One wealthy man, Jerome, had a lot to do with it. Jerome was torn between being a student of the Bible and respecting the "pagan" classics.

He dreamed that he was dragged before the judgment seat and asked who he was. When he answered, "I'm a Christian," he was told he was lying because he followed Cicero, not Christ. The judges ordered him to be scourged, whereupon he cried out for mercy and took an oath never to possess worldly books again.

Jerome went on to become a well-known Bible scholar and consultant. He was called to Rome to translate the Hebrew Bible into Latin (a Bible later called the Vulgate). In doing this major work, Jerome incorrectly translated the Hebrew word for witchcraft, *anan,* as "observing dreams." This error was apparently deliberate since Jerome was highly skilled as a translator. He correctly translated *anan* seven times as "condemning witchcraft" but mistranslated it three times as "observing dreams." Of course, this equated observing dreams with witchcraft.

Jerome's mistranslation in the Vulgate influenced beliefs for quite some time. Dreams became suspect in the Western world and were essentially nullified in Christian beliefs and practices for the next fifteen centuries.

In the same historical period, another book contributed fuel to the paranoia about dreams. Macrobius, a contemporary of Jerome's, wrote his *Commentary on the Dream of Scipio.* This book became one of the main philosophical handbooks of the Middle Ages and the best-known dream book in medieval Europe.

Little is known about Macrobius except that he may have been a Christian and that he based his writings on Cicero and the wisdom of classical Greece and Rome.

In his book on dreams he included a section about nightmares in which demons that he termed *incubus* and *succubus* attacked and possessed people sexually. As a result primarily of

Jerome's mistranslation but also likely influenced by Macrobius' writings, the Catholic church fathers no longer viewed dream interpretation as a spiritual activity but rather as a questionable superstitious practice.

The Eastern Orthodox View

The Eastern Orthodox branch of Christianity continued to value dreams as a communication with the spiritual world and the divine. The writings of Synesius of Cyrene, a fifth-century bishop, are very interesting, and radical for his time. They are similar to today's thinking.

Synesius believed that the entire universe is a unity. He theorized that dreams arise from the faculty of imagination, which he said lies halfway between reason and the world around us. This idea is close to Carl Jung's concept of the collective unconscious.

Synesius also wrote that dreams are imaginative, prophetic and problem solving, and they give hints about eternal life. However, he thought dream books were not particularly helpful in understanding individual dreams.

A Medieval Paradox

In the eleventh century, Thomas Aquinas produced his great work *Summa Theologica,* a synthesis of biblical tradition and Aristotelian philosophy. Although he examined all aspects of theological and philosophical systems, he drew no final conclusion about dreams or people's experience of the divine or the supernatural.

Aquinas recognized that some dreams come from God, but he did not encourage ordinary people to look into their dreams. Instead, his general attitude was that dreams were dangerous and rarely offered an experience of the divine. He specifically warned about the danger of demons in dreams.

Following Aquinas' writings, obsession about demons and devils became rampant. The medieval Catholic Church even pronounced that dreams were *not* of God and must be ignored. The church fathers reasoned that since the word of God was given to the church, ordinary people did not need to make contact with God through dreams. Dreams then became the hunting grounds of inquisitors. Consequently, people were not only reluctant to reveal their dreams, they actively suppressed them.

Paradoxically, Aquinas' personal experience contradicted what he had written. He came into direct relationship with God and thereafter ceased to write or dictate. When he was urged to go on, he replied, "I can do no more; such things have been revealed to me that all I have written seems as straw, and I now await the end of my life."[10] However, the damage had been done.

We can see by our review so far that the early Christians recognized dream experiences as a contact with the divine. This understanding arose from earlier cultures and had as a backdrop the combined traditions of Greek and ancient Jewish heritage.

If we were to eliminate this belief from Christianity—that we can contact the divine through our dreams—we would be calling into question the inspiration of the prophets and the divine guidance given to many figures in the Old and New Testaments. And we would also be discounting our own inner experience.

The Talmud and the Koran

Further evidence of the importance of dreams comes from the writings of other major religions. For example, the Babylonian Talmud, the compilation of Jewish tradition,[11] has 270 references to dreams. Undoubtedly the most famous of these is attributed to Rabbi Hisda: "An uninterpreted dream is like an unread letter." Another reference, offered by Rabbi Johnathan, is a meaningful spiritual insight: "A man is shown in his dreams what he thinks in his heart."

Dreams were also key to important spiritual events in the Islamic world. Islam began in the seventh century with Muhammad's dream in a cave on Hira, a hill not far from Mecca. There he was asked to read and replied that he could not. When he awoke and went outside the cave, he saw the vision of Archangel Gabriel, who told him he had been selected as Allah's messenger.

Much of the Koran, the sacred book of Islam, was delivered to the prophet Muhammad in dreams or in a trancelike state. Dreams also inspired him to embark on a number of military conquests. Muslims continue to highly value dreams and dream interpretation. They seek dream inspiration through the recitation of prayers.

A Dream Prophesies the Future of Britain

We also have a rich history of Welsh folklore and quasi-historical material about prophetic dreams, some dating to pre-Christian times. *The Chronicle of Elis Gruffydd,* a sixteenth-century manuscript now in the National Library of Wales, includes a story about Merlin's sister, Gwenddydd, who asked her brother to interpret her dreams.

One of the dreams told the following story: "I was standing in an alder grove when I saw great hosts of men coming with axes in their hands, and with these they were cutting the alder grove and felling them to the ground. And then I saw the straightest and fairest yew trees which man could imagine growing on the trunks of the alders. And then I woke."

Merlin interpreted the dream as meaning that invaders (men with axes) would come and ravage the ancient peoples of the island of Britain (alder grove). Yet from the ravaged people (the felled alder grove) would come a newer and stronger nobility (fairest yew trees). The nobility would be impoverished and forced to marry daughters of wealthy men of lesser rank (growing on the trunks of the alders).

The truth of this prophecy was borne out in the late Middle Ages after the combination of Celt, Saxon and Norman peoples produced the English race, the "newer and stronger nobility." During that era, war after war indeed impoverished the English noblemen, who married into the rapidly growing merchant class in order to restore their fortunes. Thus was the prophecy fulfilled.[12]

Dreams through the Eyes
of the Early Scientific Community

After the Middle Ages, the scientific and philosophical communities gradually began to associate dreams with scientific inquiry. As scientists began to emphasize the physical, or bodily, features of dreams, demons and devils faded into the background.

In 1690 John Locke theorized that dreams were the result of sensory input. In 1812 Benjamin Rush wrote about dreams in the first American book on psychiatry. He thought dreams were caused by a sudden mental disturbance resulting from changes in blood flow in the brain. Wilhelm Wundt, founder of the world's first psychological laboratory (in Leipzig, Germany, 1879–1880), seconded Locke's earlier opinion that sensory stimuli were the primary impetus of dreams.

By the late nineteenth century, scholars began to talk favorably about dreams. For example, in 1865 Frank Seafield wrote his classic treatise in which he stated that dreams reflected the personality of the dreamer and could be comprehended. He also wrote that when dreams were interpreted they could help solve problems and lead to a more balanced personality. He defined a cultural tone that has carried over to modern times.

Psychiatry's Influence on Dream Theory

In 1900 Sigmund Freud wrote *The Interpretation of Dreams,* which he viewed as his most important work. It was highly influential in changing the predominant view (that dreams are caused by gods, demons, or physiological processes) to the view that dreams are generated by internal conflicts.

Freud believed that dreams have a twofold purpose—preserving sleep and acting as a safety valve for unacceptable wishes. He thought dreams arose primarily to fulfill primitive, infantile wishes, such as Oedipal longings for the parent of the opposite sex. He also believed daytime happenings stimulated these wishes.

Freud theorized that analyzing repressed, distorted wishes could help people understand their unresolved urges. Thus, his well-known notion came into being—that dreams are the "royal road to the unconscious."

Freudian dream interpretation primarily uses free association. The dreamer focuses on the dream elements (the manifest content) and verbalizes whatever comes to mind. Through free-associating to the dream images, the dreamer ultimately comes to the origin of the hidden conflicts (the latent or unconscious content) revealed by the dream.

Since Freud theorized that many psychological problems were caused by repressed instinctual, libidinal urges, he often interpreted dream symbols as either sexual or aggressive in nature. His theories fit in particularly well with the cultural milieu of the Victorian Age, where women in particular were expected to hide or suppress their sexual and aggressive urges.

Although Freud believed that only the individual had the key to the meaning of his or her dreams, he also suggested there might be some form of shared symbolism among people. This idea excited the interest of one of his students, Carl Jung.

Jung broke off with his mentor to create his own theory, which focused on archetypal patterns of human nature. He called these patterns the collective unconscious, meaning the arena of collective experience shared by people of all races and cultures. Jung further departed from Freudian theory by viewing dreams as positive, normal and creative.

He believed dreams were the expression of the unconscious and served as a balancing mechanism. They helped the dreamer achieve equilibrium in waking life and a greater awareness of his or her hidden feelings. They represented sides of the personality not expressed in daily life and could also reveal inner truths that the dreamer was either unaware of or mistrusted when awake. Dreams were a key to uniting the conscious and unconscious.

In his work Jung focused on the manifest, or obvious, content of the dream. He theorized that some dream symbols were unique to the individual while others were universal. Today, Jungian therapists use dream images as metaphor in the analysis of a person's hidden issues and potentials.

Another of Freud's students, Alfred Adler, developed his theory that dreams function to preserve one's personality and sense of self-worth. For Adler, dreams were congruent with the style of life of the dreamer. They were a trustworthy approach to exploring the dreamer's personality, second only to early childhood memories.

Adler also thought of dreams as a means of rehearsing for future activities and achievements. He was just as interested in dreams that were made up as in actual dreams because he considered the imagination to be an expression of the person's style of life.

In contrast to Freud's focus on dreams as the royal road to the unconscious, Adler saw dreams as the "royal road to consciousness." Adlerian therapists consequently focus on the total experience of the dreamer rather than specifically on the unconscious strivings.

Who Is Right about the Interpretation of Your Dreams?

Contemporary dream theories draw from all of these predecessors. For example, in modern psychoanalytic thought, a dream may be uncovering underlying impulses, but its manifest content is often a direct representation of daily life. In contrast, Freud viewed dreams as nearly always presenting a distortion of hidden impulses.

Today psychoanalysts believe that dreams reflect the issues of waking life and can also further the dreamer's conscious efforts of problem solving and conflict resolution.

As psychoanalyst Dr. Ralph Yaney states, "Dreams are rarely simple, even though the content may be familiar. Dreams can be analyzed from many perspectives and are often a computer printout, as it were, of a piece of the self at a point in time attempting conflict resolution."

One major similarity between early and contemporary psychoanalysts is the use of free association. It is a basic therapeutic tool for uncovering the dreamer's feelings and reactions to the daytime events that may have stimulated the dream.

Other contemporary therapists of different theoretical persuasions also use free association, along with the process of developing insight, to unravel the meaning of their clients' dreams.

What about dream symbols? Many analysts today believe that symbols are the result of our mind's general ability to create likeness and metaphor. Thus, when we free-associate to our dream symbols, we develop an understanding of them and consequently the meaning of a dream.

Dream dictionaries, so popular today, are thought to be of limited use because they suggest only the culturally common meanings of different images.

What can we learn from all of this? We see that dreams have always been a part of the human condition and the understanding of dreams has been unfolding over thousands of years.

Who is right about the interpretation of your dreams? I believe *you* are. A good analyst can help, but no one else knows you as well as you do. You hold the keys to your own personal dream symbolism.

You are the dreamer, the dream and your own dream analyst. As you unfold the meaning of your dream messages, you discover the mysterious process of self-revelation. It's an exciting journey!

CHAPTER THREE

Physiology of Sleeping and Dreaming

You see things; and you say, "Why?"
But I dream things that never were;
and I say, "Why not?"

—GEORGE BERNARD SHAW
Back to Methuselah

*P*erhaps you are saying to yourself, "Where is the scientific basis for all of these mystical experiences and psychological theories?" Actually, we now know from modern sleep-lab studies that everyone dreams when sleeping. We also know that deprivation of the dream-sleep stages can produce serious psychological dysfunction.

Dreaming seems to be a built-in mechanism for processing the events of the day, particularly the upsetting or confusing happenings and any conflicting thoughts, emotions or physical reactions to those happenings. We also process old memories and conflicts in our dreams, issues that we are still harboring because we have not consciously resolved them. The dream process, then, is seen by many researchers as a way of maintaining psychological health and well-being.

How Does All of This Work?

According to research on sleep and sleep deprivation, as we go into sleep our brain waves gradually slow down. We move from a state of wakefulness, the beta brain-wave pattern, to a slower brain-wave pattern, the alpha state. This is the period when our eyelids begin to droop and we find ourselves drifting back and forth in a kind of reverie, in and out of beta and alpha several times before we slip into deeper levels of sleep.

Over the next few moments our brain waves continue slowing down, and we drift fairly quickly through the alpha state into the slower brain-wave pattern of theta. Theta is a stage of deep sleep where we experience a vague type of dreaming or thought process, which scientists call non-REM, or NREM. It is interesting that the mind, even in deep sleep, never seems to be entirely still.

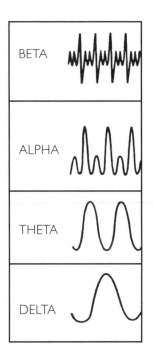

We move rather quickly through theta into delta, the slowest brain-wave pattern and deepest level of consciousness. At one time researchers believed that dreams did not occur in the delta state, but more recent studies indicate that some form of dreaming is associated with every level of sleep.

Some thirty to forty minutes later, our brain waves begin to speed up and we drift back from delta through theta and into the alpha state again. At this point, our bodies become quite still, as though we are focused on watching some drama (exactly what we are doing), for in this stillness we are experiencing REM sleep.

Although our eyelids are closed, our eyes begin to move quickly, signaling that we are actively dreaming. In fact, this dream period is named REM after the accompanying "rapid eye movement." In sleep-lab studies, people awakened during REM sleep are able to recall and describe their dreams.

Cycles of Dreaming through the Night

After we have been in REM sleep for five to ten minutes, we reverse course and move back through theta into delta, where we remain until our deep-sleep cycle is complete. At that point we return once more to the alpha state to begin a second dream cycle.

Approximately every hour and a half, we cycle through these stages of sleep. During the early hours of sleep, we spend more time in the deeper stages and only about ten minutes in REM sleep. As the night goes on, we spend less time in the slower brain-wave states (theta and delta) and more time in REM. As we approach awakening in the morning, we may be spending up to an hour in our last cycle of REM sleep. Thus, when we sleep the frequently recommended 8 hours at night we likely have four REM periods, comprising approximately 20 to 25 percent of our total sleep time, or 1½ to 2 hours.[1]

Daydreams

In addition to the nightly dream cycle, some type of dream activity seems to be present in the waking state as well. For example, I have observed with clients and myself that the content of daydreams is similar to that of night dreams and, in fact, can be analyzed in much the same way.

I have also noticed that children spend a lot of time daydreaming, particularly those in difficult life situations. When they daydream—playing out their fantasies or creating imaginary friends—they are dramatizing their hopes and wishes or processing troublesome events in their lives.

In therapy sessions with children, we set up an environment for their play activity with puppets, dolls, sandboxes, drawing, painting, modeling clay and computer games. These activities help children express their imagination, resolve conflicts and heal inner pain and confusion—much as we do in our dreams.

The Good Fairy Heals a Child's Nightmare

I remember one five-year-old girl who had nightmares about a monster hiding in the family coat-closet. In her home life, she had an alcoholic father, who terrorized the family when he was drunk. In therapy Rachel drew rainbows and talked to her Good Fairy. She asked the fairy to "wave a magic wand and make the monster go away." This was her way of symbolizing and trying to cope with the family situation.

In this particular case, the family's concern about Rachel's nightmares led to her father going into treatment for his alcoholism. When he stopped drinking and terrorizing the family, Rachel's monster went away. She told me, "I just knew the Good Fairy could make the monster go away!" What a blessing Rachel's hopes and dreams were for her family.

Rachel's imaginative play was similar to what we do when we dream or daydream. These activities—dreaming, daydreaming and imaginative play—are all natural ways in which we portray and resolve our life happenings.

More on Alpha Waves and the Dream State

When we look more closely at the alpha-wave pattern, where REM sleep occurs, we see that it is actually made up of several mini-levels, each having its own special purpose. Some of these levels are associated with waking activities, such as meditating or daydreaming.

The first mini-level is alpha one, or al-beta, a combination of alpha and beta. This is the level of brain activity when we are daydreaming or brainstorming. The brain waves have slowed to 12 to 14 cycles per second. The body is relaxed and the mind quiet. At the same time, the mind is aware of physical sensations and is in touch with the alpha level of the intuitive mind.

In this alpha-one state, we are in a balanced combination of right- and left-brain input, known as the rhythm of genius. We may come up with new ideas, ingenious inventions or creative solutions to problems during this level of brain activity.[2]

Although not yet confirmed by formal research, either alpha one or the next mini-level, alpha two, is the likely stage where we tune in to the spiritual arena of the universal mind or cosmic consciousness. In psychosynthesis, this arena is called the superconscious.

Roberto Assagioli, a student of Carl Jung and founder of psychosynthesis, describes the superconscious as the inner region from which "we receive our higher intuitions and inspirations—artistic, philosophical or scientific, ethical 'imperatives' and urges to humanitarian and heroic action. It is the source of the higher feelings, such as altruistic love; of genius and of the states of contemplation, illumination, and ecstasy."[3]

As we move into alpha two, the slightly slower range of 10 to 12 cycles per second, our mind seems to be in a delicate balance between waking and sleeping. We are relatively un-aware of outer sensory phenomena but our mind is inwardly aware, alert, sensitive and extremely receptive to transcendent thoughts and feelings.

During this stage we may daydream, meditate, experience a flash of insight or sense of intuitive knowing, or receive a numinous vision. However, we do not hold this state very long because of the delicate balance between alpha one and alpha two. We move rapidly on to sleep or suddenly startle into wakefulness.

The alpha-two phase seems to be the gateway to lucid dreaming. In a lucid dream we are aware of ourselves as we dream or enter an altered state of consciousness (see chapter 10). Our sense of clarity and awareness can reach new heights and we may even consciously change what is going on in our dream.

For example, a client of mine met a gangster in a dream. Instead of shrinking from his threats, she simply asked him, "Who are you?" When he said, "I'm the bully," she told him, "Go away. I'm not about to be bullied by you." And he disap-peared.

The slightly slower alpha-three level is associated with deep meditation, trance and hypnotic states as well as with light sleep. The brain waves range from about 8 to 10 cycles per second with spurts dipping lower or higher at intervals. Often in alpha three we think we are awake, since we may hear sounds like someone talking in another room, cars going by outside or children playing in the yard. However, if anything startles us, we suddenly move to beta with a jerk, awakening with a sense of shock or surprise because we didn't realize we had been asleep.

At only a slightly lower cycling, we reach alpha four. The dreams we have at this stage seem to be stored in the subconscious. A forgotten dream, however, may suddenly surface during meditation or as we daydream. Perhaps you have had this experience. How does it occur?

Remember that in normal waking life, we are in the beta-wave state and not in contact with our alpha meditations or dreams unless we have already brought them to conscious awareness. When we meditate, however, we move into one of the mini-levels of the alpha state, the arena of most of the dreams we remember.

We might surmise that our experiences in different levels of the alpha state interweave, especially when they are similar in content or share an emotional connection that the dreamer needs to understand. So when we are in the alpha state, daydreaming or meditating, a dream memory can rise to our conscious awareness.

REM-Sleep Deprivation

In one study investigating the value of REM sleep, students being tested were allowed to have a full eight hours of sleep but were awakened each time a dream would begin. This process had a powerful impact on the students. After only three days, some of them had developed major excitability, irritability, abnormal behavior patterns, disorientation, hallucinations and, in a few cases, signs of psychosis. The experience was so disturbing to one young man that he refused to continue participating after one night of dream deprivation.

When the REM-deprivation test was over, the students who had remained in the study were given a normal, uninterrupted night's sleep. Thereafter they returned to their normal behavior, but all of them spent much more time in REM sleep during the next few nights. The students seemed to be subconsciously trying to catch up on their REM-dream time as fast as they could.[4]

From the reported research we understand that REM sleep is highly important to our mental processes and overall sense of balance and well-being. Dream studies have also demonstrated that drugs, alcohol, sleeping pills and certain medicines, such as antihistamines, tend to keep the consciousness in the very deepest level, delta, thus preventing REM sleep.

Dr. William Dement, a pioneer in sleep research and sleep disorders, has written many articles and books on his findings. In his book *Some Must Watch While Some Must Sleep,* Dement relates that the symptoms of REM-deprived subjects include difficulty in concentrating. He also states his belief that delirium tremens (DTs)—a condition of violent delirium with tremors, associated with excessive and prolonged use of alcohol —is "an accumulation of deprived REM."[5]

Factors Influencing Dream Recall

Psychologists and psychiatrists have proposed a number of modern theories to explain dreams: wish fulfillment, the preservation of sleep, physiological stimuli, and processing of information and emotions from daytime events.

Today, most researchers agree that dreams reflect concerns from waking life and help people integrate information and cope with varied emotions. Studies of content analysis validate these beliefs. They indicate a significant correspondence between what we dream about and our preoccupations when we are awake.

Why do we remember some dreams and not others? What are the factors at play here? Can we enhance our ability to recall our dreams?

Dreams that are very clear, novel, bizarre, vivid, active, lengthy and emotionally charged are more likely to be remembered than "bland" dreams. The final dreams of the night, as we might expect, are the ones we most likely remember. When we rehearse our dreams immediately upon awakening, we aid our recall of them.

Research indicates that a number of other factors influence our dream recall: the sleep environment (for example, quiet or noisy); our own sleeping habits (uninterrupted or waking up several times); how we awaken (naturally or by something startling us); the stage of sleep from which we awaken; and how the dream report is collected.[6]

Women Recall Dreams More Often Than Men

Some dreams have been very common among people all over the world, such as dreams of falling, flying, being chased or appearing nude. Other dreams are more specific to a particular culture or time in history. (In this chapter we are looking at dream research completed in the United States after 1950.)

An extensive study of one thousand dreams, conducted in 1966, found that the dreams of both men and women seemed to be influenced by marital status, racial and ethnic background, and socioeconomic status. Researchers found that women's dreams had more emotional content and they recalled dreams an average of 8 percent more often than men.

Men's dreams involved more male characters, outdoor settings, tools, weapons, physical aggression, sexuality, strangers and animals than did women's. Women's dreams had more female characters, indoor settings, verbal activities, clothes, familiar people, children and babies than men's dreams.

Interestingly, subsequent studies conducted in the 1980s and 1990s showed that women's dreams are changing. In keeping with the shifting roles and expectations for women over the last forty years, women's dreams are now reflecting their expanded role in the workplace.[7]

I have seen this shift in my own psychotherapy practice. In the 1960s, most of the women in therapy with me dreamed of themselves in the traditional roles of home and family. My women clients today dream about problems with bosses or co-workers, frustrations about working conditions or issues associated with their role as managers.

A central conclusion from much of the research is that all dreams appear to be meaningful, consistent with our personality and connected to events in our lives. In addition, they are metaphorical attempts to deal with our life experiences and emotional preoccupations.

Each of us has this vast inner world of creative genius. At night we play out our life dramas. We safely express our tender or unruly emotions. We develop insights that may carry over into our daytime activities. When we explore our dreams and apply their lessons and guidance to the situations of the day, they become a valuable resource.

CHAPTER FOUR

Interpreting Symbols and Metaphors

*Life and dreams are leaves
of the same book.*

—ARTHUR SCHOPENHAUER

*W*hat about brief snatches of a dream or seemingly mundane dreams related to waking-life experiences? How do we interpret them? How can they help us in our daily life?

Sometimes our dreams help us handle the feelings and impressions of the day that we haven't processed and may not even be aware of consciously. They allow us to discharge unpleasant and unacceptable feelings about ourselves or our circumstances.

At other times our dreams may be showing us a mixed blend of our positive and negative aspects, thereby giving us a truer picture of who we really are and allowing us to experience our more positive and creative sides.

When we interpret our dreams from these points of view, we understand that each person, object, place and event in a dream, or even a brief snatch of a dream, symbolizes an aspect of our own life. Thus, we dramatize our hopes and desires, fears, regrets, victories and defeats. Our dreams allow us to express all of who we are and all of who we may become.

A contemporary approach to dream interpretation, a combination of classical and modern methods, has the dreamer identify and then role play each element of the dream. This approach allows the more hidden parts of our consciousness involved in the dream to surface.

We focus on each dream element as a part of our conscious or unconscious self that is seeking expression. As we do this, we begin to see how these parts interrelate in the dream and how they impact our waking life. In this vein, Fritz Perls, founder of Gestalt therapy, believed that dreams are a way of integrating the disparate parts of our personalities.

In our dreams, all the parts of our self become players in a drama staged by our Higher Self and our soul. The purpose is to offer us a special message or lesson that we need to learn in order to resolve a problem in our life or fulfill an aspect of our soul's destiny. Sometimes the dream reveals attitudes or motivations that we have taken on unconsciously from our childhood family.

Three Unique Mother Dreams

As we look at the following three dreams, notice how each one is presented in imagery unique to that dreamer and how both positive and negative aspects of the dreamer are represented.*

Christy. This young woman's dream glyph revealed a conflict about how best to fulfill her inner sense of spiritual direction: "I'm watching a woman who is looking for a job in the presence of a psychoanalyst. She is sitting in a chair filling out a form. She writes that she is supposed to do heavenly deeds. The female psychoanalyst communes telepathically

---

*I have changed the names, places and some of the details to protect the anonymity of the individuals whose dreams I analyze in this book.

with me and says, 'How can anyone write down "heavenly deeds?"' I want to defend the woman and what she has written, so I say, 'Heavenly deeds can be very humble.'"

Christy's associations to "heavenly deeds" revealed her inner desire to do God's work on Earth. She identified with the woman looking for the job and defended her desire to do heavenly deeds as being "humble," implying that the analyst might think it prideful.

The presence and comment of the analyst implies that at some level Christy is worried that she is crazy and prideful. The condescension of the female analyst was reminiscent of Christy's mother and her rebuking attitude.

It also represented Christy's own ambivalence about her desire to do heavenly deeds. Thus, the dream represented Christy's inner conflict and her sense of insecurity about standing on her own and pursuing her soul's spiritual mission in the face of her mother's disapproval.

How did Christy summarize her dream message? "I need to get beyond reacting to and internalizing my mother's attitudes. I need to get on with my spiritual work. To do this, I need to transform the shadow [analyst/mother] part of me,* trust my inner guidance, ask Almighty God to keep me humble, and find a loving way of helping people."

Ginny. This client had a very different set of symbols, although her central issue was also her relationship with her mother. Ginny dreamed about sharks. She awoke feeling

---

*According to Carl Jung's teachings, the shadow archetype is the dark side of our human nature.

trapped, claustrophobic and panicky.

In her associations she saw sharks as cold, calculating killers, and immediately realized, "That's my anger. I can get that mad at my mother." She remembered looking at the shark's face and thinking, "I know I'm going to die."

Ginny was identified with the terrorized victim side of herself who could not get away from her own sharklike anger. Her dream message was, "My anger and vengeance can kill me."

In our session she resolved to stop playing victim, to face her anger and work on transforming it. Her vision was of changing the shark into a dolphin, which equated with positive power and grace.

To reinforce her resolutions, she began a daily spiritual ritual, affirming, "I choose to surrender my anger. I ask God for forgiveness. I forgive myself and I forgive my mother. I accept God's gift of positive power and grace." Of course, it was not as easy to do as to say. But Ginny understood that she was psychologically killing herself with her anger.

In her daily life she has put into practice what she learned from her dream. She is making her own decisions. She is getting to the point where she can listen to her mother attack a decision she has made and stand up for herself. Now she is working on being somewhat gracious in the process. And she feels good about her progress.

Pauline. Another client, Pauline, highly resented being on the receiving end of her mother's power plays but had a different dream symbol to represent her anger. She described her dream: "I pulled up in my vehicle in a large parking lot. A big black truck pulled up beside me, between my vehicle and a cream-colored wall. I realize this is the playground area of a school I attended as a child. I get out of my car. All of a sudden, I see it rolling backwards, out of control."

For Pauline the car is her power, her mobility. The scene of the dream is a school she had attended as a child, which had a large paved area where the children used to skate and play. The presence of the black vehicle was ominous—reminding her of how she felt when her mother became angry. As she said, "I'd be scared, frustrated and angry myself."

The wall, solid and lighter in color than everything else in the dream, represented her light side, her fun side. She said, "In contrast to the black truck, it's like seeing the light. The black truck represents what I have taken in of my mother's anger as well as my own, and it's sitting between me and the light."

The car going backwards, out of control, represents Pauline's power and mobility. "When I get angry," she said with a sigh, "I'm going backwards and out of control. It's the most destructive part of me." In this dream she emphasizes her anger by showing it to herself in two ways: as the car moving backwards without her in it and as the big black truck coming between her and her light, fun side.

Pauline had an important realization: "I suppose my not being in the car and the black truck being driven by someone else means I'm abdicating my responsibility. Which is true. When something frustrates me these days, I either fume or let 'er rip! It goes back to not expressing anger as a child because my mother wouldn't allow it. I remember being very frustrated with my parents when I was attending this school but I couldn't express it."

In Pauline's family only her mother and father were allowed to get angry. When Pauline got out on her own, she realized how frustrated and angry she had been, but she didn't know what to do about it. Through the dream and the interpretation of it, Pauline is bringing these old feelings to the surface so that she can resolve them and move on.

I asked Pauline what she thought the dream's message was. After thinking for a moment she replied, "I am abdicating responsibility for my mobility and power. I am going backwards and allowing a truckload of anger to get in the way of seeing the light and expressing my fun side. I'm saying to myself, 'Lighten up!'"

Her therapy homework was to do exactly that: get into the driver's seat of her life and lighten up instead of engaging the old momentum of anger. Seeing the light was a twofold message for her: (1) the need to transform her anger and frustration through invoking spiritual light and (2) the need to see some humor in difficult situations.

All of these clients had similar issues. But they dreamed about them differently and dealt with them in their own unique, constructive ways. Individuality is our most precious asset. Your dream is your own drama. Your way of processing it is unique to who you are, and your solution will represent your own soul's creative bent.

A Humorous Approach to Power and Mobility

Did you know that your soul and Higher Self can be playful when trying to get your attention and guide you to a deeper understanding? We tend to think of dreams as being rather serious in nature. But while the message may be quite serious, the dream imagery can be playful or humorous.

Debbie had a need to claim her power and mobility in a positive way. She also has a remarkable sense of humor, so she played out her drama in a humorous way:

"I'm almost to the top of a mountain that has a dome-shaped top. I still have to cross a chasm, so I rig a rope ladder to get across. Then I'm looking up at myself crossing the chasm on the rope. I'm thinking, 'This is dangerous. My admiring such a feat is not warranted.' Suddenly the rope ladder dissolves, and I'm slammed against the mountain. A man pulls me up, feet first. I decide the whole thing is stupid and stomp down the mountain. Native American warriors are at hand. At nightfall, I sneak into their camp and steal two chickens and one rooster. I try to put the chickens back, and then I wake up."

Debbie's associations brought out the following picture: She is uneasy that she will get out of balance when she tries to cross the chasm, the deep valley of the unconscious. She is venturing over dangerous ground. The dissolving rope ladder indicates that her link with protection is weak. Being slammed into the mountain is a dramatic confrontation with reality. The man pulling her up, feet first, is her masculine side showing her in a comical way that she is upside down in her thinking and needs to lead with her understanding (feet often symbolize understanding).

When she decides the whole thing is stupid and comes stomping down, she is annoyed and aware that she had been doing a false-heroism stunt, representing a daredevil consciousness that she herself realizes is dumb. She needs to get her feet back on the ground, which she does symbolically by stomping down the mountain.

Debbie respects the way Native Americans live close to their instincts and to the earth. She also has a warrior spirit in the positive sense of forging ahead and not being deterred by anything. Her stealing the chickens and rooster from the warriors and trying to put the chickens back is a humorous message to herself. The rooster symbolizes her "cock-a-doodle-do" masculine daredevil strut. It's combined with "I'm not keeping the chicken part of myself."

Shorthand dream message: "Neither a chicken nor a daredevil be!"

Debbie realizes she has a certain pride in being macho that can lead her into dangerous territory. She has made great strides in reclaiming her power and effectiveness in constructive ways. This means being in touch with her instinctive warrior nature while keeping her feet on the ground. That translates to being daring but not daredevilish, thinking things through before leaping into them, and avoiding unnecessary risks. It's a big agenda for her. Her sense of humor, though, is a major asset. While she often takes two steps forward and one backward, she laughs at herself and keeps on going.

Is Every Dream Worth Analyzing?

Some people tell me they don't think their dreams are worth analyzing because they either have no clear content or make no sense. Yet dreams are almost always a message from you to you, and it is something you want to know. I believe all dreams can be analyzed fruitfully. Some may just take more digging than others to uncover the message.

As an example I'd like to relate a therapy session with Mark. He told me he did not put a lot of stock in dream analysis, and all he could remember about his dream was that it took place at night. I began by asking him, "What does 'night' make you think of?" He said, "It's dark."

"What does 'dark' make you think of?" He said, "Unknown."

I asked him to keep telling me what each association made him think of until he ran out of associations. Mark's entire series of associations to the dream were "night," "dark," "unknown," "shadowy figures," "scary," "helpless," "victim," "I'm not in control."

By the end of the chain of associations he had arrived at the concept most personally relevant for him. The issue for Mark was "control." To another person, "night" might have meant something entirely different.

I asked Mark to look at the parts of himself that the dream associations might represent. He told me that when he thought of "dark," he thought of "danger." He put "danger" and "shadowy figures" together to mean his negative shadow side, a part of himself that he didn't like because it could act out in a violent way.[1]

"Unknown" had him stumped for a bit, but then he said, "Well, I don't like the unknown either. It's actually kind of scary. It's like shadowboxing. You don't know who your opponent is. That must be why the dream makes me feel kind of helpless and victimized."

He was getting excited now as he began to get the full understanding of this brief glyph of a dream. He said, "A part of me is scared of being a victim of my dark side, scared of what my tendency to violence can do to me. If I keep behaving that way, I could end up in jail. That's where my temper could land me. And I'd sure feel like a victim then!"

Mark's dream was all about how he was victimizing himself through playing out his dark side. His own violence had reached the point that it scared him. He had come up with the associations and thereby had come to understand what this dark side was doing to him.

Mark went on, "Now I'm thinking about that 'I'm not in control' thing. I think that applies both to my violent side and to my victim side. I'm telling myself that whether I'm being violent or feeling helpless, I'm not in control of my life. So now what do I do about that?"

I asked, "Could the violence represent your out-of-control power side? And the victim, your soft side that gets the worst of it?"

Mark looked thoughtful. "Yes, that would fit. You remember my dad was always in a rage and my mom always playing victim. I suppose that fits in, too. I don't think I learned positive ways to handle tough situations."

I responded, "How about you as a man today? How would you want to handle a tough situation that both scares you and triggers your violence?"

Mark was quick to respond, "I'd want to stand up for myself in a strong way without losing my cool."

"Okay," I said, "what would be a strong way of standing up for yourself without losing your cool?"

Mark was silent for a few moments. "Okay, I've got it. I know what this dream thing is all about now. My boss has been on my case to get this project finished, and I've been dragging my feet because I'm not sure he's going to like the way I've approached it. I've been alternating between feeling belligerent toward him about it and worrying about the way he'll react when he sees the results."

I asked, "How do you feel about the way you approached the project?"

He responded, "I feel good about the work I've done. But I'm not sure he is going to like it. Okay, okay, I get it. I'm either going to have to stand on what I've done and make the best presentation I'm capable of, or I'm going to be running out of time on it anyway."

"Mark, what would it take for you to trust yourself on this one and let the chips fall where they may, whether the boss likes it or not?"

"I might do just that. Maybe that's what this dream glyph is trying to tell me. I'm shadowboxing with the unknown of what the boss is going to say. And the only way to make it known is to make the presentation. If he likes it, great! If he doesn't, I guess we aren't on the same page anyway. If he wants to fire me for that, so be it."

I was hearing just a bit of the old belligerence there and commented, "I wonder if you would get further if you just stuck to making a terrific presentation of the idea you believe in—instead of second guessing what the boss is or isn't going to say and then getting kind of belligerent about it ahead of time?"

Mark laughed, "Okay, you've got me there. I'll let you know what happens. It's kind of surprising what a brief dream glyph can bring up, isn't it?"

"One more thought, Mark," I said. "I think you are going to need to team up the positive masculine and feminine sides of yourself in order to pull this off. To me, positive teamwork could mean the balance of empowerment and compassion. If you were to claim the empowerment of the victim and some compassion on the side of the dark controller, you would have a winning team."

Mark was quick to retort, "Does that mean I'm supposed to have compassion for the boss?"

I responded, "I don't know. You tell me. Is he really the dark controller? At the very least, you could have some compassion for yourself by lightening up a bit."

He loosened up again, "Well, actually, the boss is under the corporate gun to get this project off the ground, so I can understand why he's been on my case. I have been stalling a bit. Okay, I'll give it a go at being diplomatic and let you know what happens."

Mark made his presentation, went back and forth with his boss in his most diplomatic way, and scored a victory. The project flew and so did Mark's self-esteem. He told me afterward, "So much for dreams not being worth analyzing. I'm going to pay very close attention to those dream glyphs from now on. Maybe I'll start remembering more of the details. That could be very interesting."

As Mark's experience demonstrates, we can gain profound personal insights when we analyze and understand our dream messages. Even a brief glyph can be rich in information and guidance.

I view every dream as being a message from the different dimensions of who we are—the archetypes of the unconscious; our subconscious motivations, thoughts and feelings; superconscious inspirations; and the hopes and dreams of our soul and Higher Self. The dreamer is meant to understand and apply the dream's message in waking life.

In Mark's case, he needed to empower himself in a threatening work situation. At the same time he also needed to be compassionate toward himself and both forthright and compassionate with his boss. He ended up doing all three.

I believe that the third of our life we spend sleeping is very much a creative process once we understand it. We show ourselves the breadth of our motivations and attitudes, unresolved issues, emotional victories and defeats, thought patterns that aren't congruent with who we want to be, and patterns of behavior that are problematic in some way. Our soul, hand in hand with our Higher Self, becomes our coach, instructing us to look at the good, the bad and the ugly within—and to do something about it.

Yes, indeed, this kind of work does take practice. But it is worth it! Dream work provides a viable route to claiming our higher qualities and getting acquainted with the person we are meant to become. In so doing we gradually transform ourselves and enrich our lives and the lives of those around us. By the way, did I tell you? Mark got a raise!

Two Levels of Interpretation

A useful approach in dream interpretation is to analyze a dream on two different levels. First, a dream represents actual happenings in our lives, as when we go hiking in the woods and dream that night about making it to the top of Mount Everest.

Second, the dream also serves to spotlight an aspect of our life that we are overlooking, neglecting or mishandling. For example, climbing to the top of Mount Everest might be a metaphor for a sense of insecurity about making it to the top in our job. In the dream, our desire to make it to the top gets fulfilled.

Thus, the same dream may be understood on the level of its obvious content or interpreted on a deeper subjective level where it becomes a metaphor to express underlying feelings, motivations and attitudes toward life.

We often do our emotional homework through our dreams. During the day, we may be too busy and preoccupied to attend to our emotions, so at night we dream about them.

And we may resolve emotional tangles that could have disrupted the next day. When we pay attention to the emotional content of our dreams, we have the opportunity to resolve our deeper feelings and recover more quickly from life's emotional crises.

A Past-Life Experience

When we investigate our dreams at the deeper level, we find that our emotional reactions not only go back to childhood but may also relate to a past life.

For example, Melissa, a client of mine, was working through some very difficult emotional reactions. Her dream glyph was seemingly benign but actually loaded with emotion. Her associations revealed elements of happenings from early childhood (one level of exploration) and neglected emotions that were more difficult to understand and resolve (a deeper level of exploration that took her back to a major past-life experience).

Melissa described her dream: "I'm crawling through a tunnel of bright white snow. I come to an area where there are mounds of snow. I can barely squeeze through. I get to a place where it's a wall of snow. I can't go any further. I turn around to go back. And then I wake up."

I asked Melissa for her associations to her dream. She responded, "I could get claustrophobic in a place like that but I didn't feel that way in the dream. It reminds me of how as kids we played in this big drainpipe near my house. It was a hiding place. We'd hide from our parents. We'd get to the end and crawl back the other way. It was fun."

For Melissa, hiding from her parents was like being in her own secret place. It was also like hiding from God, for the bright white snow symbolized the bright light of awareness. The snow also represented a frozen emotional state at the subconscious level—being almost paralyzed by fear, feeling out of touch with her emotions and unable to control their expression.

Melissa fears being overwhelmed by her emotions so she freezes them. The wall of snow indicates that she is blocked; she can't go any further. She has to go back to resolve her issues. The main message is that unless she thaws her emotions, she can't go forward, and turning around to go back through the tunnel is going backwards.

The positive aspect of going backwards means to retrace the origin of her fears and wake up to a problem. Interestingly, at this point Melissa wakes up and remembers the dream.

As we worked through her associations, Melissa realized the dream was more than a dream, that it symbolized a past-life experience in which she separated herself from her spiritual origins. In her words, "I think this whole thing goes back to when I left off from God in ancient times and felt alone, abandoned and separated from God. Just thinking about that scares the living daylights out of me.

"I realize my sense of separation from God is coming to the surface. In a way I'm glad, because I want to resolve it. But I don't like feeling it. I'm going to bring this whole thing to the surface, get through it and really surrender it, instead of just thinking about surrendering it. I'll need to open my heart and soul to God instead of hiding out in my snow tunnel, which really isn't so much fun after all."

Anima and Animus Projections

Let's take a look at our masculine and feminine sides—which we all have. Carl Jung described the masculine and feminine within us in terms of specific archetypes: the anima (the feminine component of a man's personality) and the animus (the masculine component of a woman's personality).

In our dreams these archetypes portray the other side of ourselves. In a woman's dream, the male characters represent different aspects of her animus, her masculine psychological tendencies. In a man's dream, the female figures personify dimensions of his anima, his feminine psychological tendencies.

The anima and animus appear as dream characters who express unrecognized attributes or psychological patterns. We learn a lot about our hidden nature by observing and interpreting these appearances of our inner "other half."[2]

Here is a dream of a young man, Jonathan, which exposes his dilemma about how to handle his unbridled passions. They are a product of both his negative masculine self (his shadow) and his feminine side (his anima). In addition, Jonathan has an issue with boundaries and a pattern of getting into codependent relationships (where each person reinforces the dysfunctional behavior of the other). Consciously, though, he is earnestly seeking a genuine, loving relationship.

Jonathan described his dream as follows: "I am on a beach with two women who are like sisters to me. They are fishing.

I'm watching them. A different woman, one I've been attracted to, walks over to me. She kisses me and invites me to come with her to her car.

"There's another guy in her car; he's in love with her. She's going after both of us, and the other guy is really hurt about it. I ask her to drive me back. And I tell her I don't like her being unfaithful like that. She turns it around and blames me for all the relationships I've ever had. Then I realize I am blaming her for my problems in past relationships that haven't worked out.

"When I woke up, I decided to write letters to the ladies I have dated who were unfaithful to me. After I wrote those letters, I realized I had actually created these problems myself because of my expectations and illusions and not keeping my boundaries. So I burned the letters instead of sending them."

I asked Jonathan to free-associate to the people and elements in his dream. The fishing experience represented good moments from childhood where he felt calm and centered. He said, "Fishing is like magic to me." The women fishing represented his positive feminine side (positive anima) that had no agenda. He doubles this positive side in his dream to emphasize its importance.

Being kissed and invited to the car of the seductive woman represents the wayward passions that Jonathan has projected onto the women in his life. He associates the car as a place to make out and realizes that he has expended a lot of sexual energy at the expense of his soul and spirit.*

---

*In keeping with esoteric traditions, I consider the soul to be the feminine polarity of our spiritual being and the spirit the masculine polarity.

The woman who invites him to her car represents the negative face of his anima. On the one hand she seems to be inviting and loving. On the other hand, she is actually blaming and unforgiving when she doesn't get what she wants. The man in the car represents his lovesick, dying-to-be-loved wounded masculine. This is a passive shadow side and represents his unruly passions and lack of boundaries.

Jonathan told me he enjoys being adventurous in relationships. However, he gets himself into trouble by being overly sympathetic and trying to take care of his girlfriends instead of respecting their ability to take care of themselves. Due to his eagerness to please a woman, he ends up giving himself away. She gets dependent on him; he ends up taking care of her. Then the relationship ends up in codependency instead of being one of mutual give and take. At that point Jonathan wants out.

All of this relates to Jonathan's childhood relationship with his mother. She has always been his best friend, and he has always tried to support her. As a child, he would forgo his own desires in order to meet her needs. In his adult relationships with women, he is unconsciously driven by the same need to please the mother. This carryover from childhood essentially results in his mother being a hidden partner in his adult relationships.

Yet when Jonathan forgoes his own desires to meet the needs of the woman in his life, it backfires. He feels trapped into meeting her needs. He doesn't really want the woman he's in love with to be so dependent on him, yet he unwittingly sets it up by pleasing her and ignoring his own needs and desires. Jonathan wants to resolve these dynamics so that he can create a healthy, lasting love relationship with a woman.

What is Jonathan's dream telling him? In the first place, he is showing himself that he needs to understand and transform the unbounded passions of his masculine and feminine natures.

By implication, as he maintains his boundaries and takes responsibility for his own thoughts, feelings, and actions in his relationships with women, he will come closer to being the man he really wants to be. He will reclaim his anima projections and avoid taking too much responsibility for a woman he loves. Then he will be able to do his part in nurturing a genuine heart-and-soul connection with a woman.

Jonathan clearly wants to establish such a relationship of mutual respect and caring. He is also serious about mastering his passions. Although he is a well-balanced person in many ways, his passions have been his Achilles' heel.

He is making progress on reclaiming his anima projections. And he is trying to be totally aware of what he is doing when he projects his own issues into a relationship with a woman. He is working on getting to know a woman he likes for who she really is instead of for who he wants her to be.

Jonathan is also taking responsibility for himself by harnessing his passions instead of allowing them free rein. His growing awareness and self-mastery are gradually transforming his tendency to oversympathize and get stuck in thorny relationships.

Dream Analysis: Four Stages

As you may notice from the examples I have given, dream analysis as I do it is a four-stage process: exploration, insight, direction for change and action plan.

- **Exploration**

First we explore the dream. The dreamer free-associates to each of the dream elements, experiencing and labeling the feelings.

Because dreams connect waking events and past memories, they can only be understood by processing them thoroughly. When we free-associate to the dream images and the emotions aroused by them, we reactivate the drama so that it can be restructured.

The exploration stage, then, proceeds through three steps: revisiting and retelling the dream, associating sequentially to the dream images, and re-experiencing the emotions.

- **Insight**

Concepts about dreams have changed a lot from the ancient belief that they were external and sent by gods or demons. Today, therapists believe dreams reflect the life issues and thoughts and emotions of the dreamer.

Consequently, there is purpose in the dream. The dream may be highlighting conflicts to be understood, insights to be gained, linkages to be made to either current happenings or past experiences.

At the insight stage, we put together what we have learned about the conscious and unconscious self through the dream.

The raw material for this stage is the initial dream, associations to the images, whatever emotional arousal is attached to the images, and the links to present-day or past situations.

When we go through the process of exploring our dream images and associations to them, we gain insight. We discover underlying attitudes, motivations, and disparities between our values and behavior.

As a result, we may tap into our higher consciousness and pursue an understanding of the more enigmatic or symbolic aspects of the dream. This search often brings to awareness higher hopes and dreams that are opposed by ingrained character traits or habit patterns.

Thus, we can analyze and understand our dreams as representing many different levels of our being: We may simply accept a dream as an interesting inner experience. We may look at its connection to past or present happenings in our lives.

We may investigate the "players" in the dream as nuances of our surface personality or the depths of our character. We may consider how a dream relates to our spirituality—the inner dimensions of our soul and Higher Self. And there is always interplay back and forth between exploration and insight.

As you go through this process of self-analysis and seek to gain insight into your dream drama, ask yourself, "Why am I giving myself this dream? What is the dream message?"

- **Direction for Change**
  Insight without action would be sterile. Based on our self-analysis, we change our perspective. A new direction either appears naturally or evolves out of ongoing inner reflection or

a discussion between the dreamer and the therapist.

The dreamer may decide what kind of changes he or she wants to make in handling particular circumstances. For instance, the dreamer may want to change attitudes, mind-sets, emotional reactions and behaviors as implied in the dream.

• **Action Plan**

The last step is to create and follow through with an action plan. My clients tell me that the benefits of dream analysis and following through with an action plan are very real. They have been able to change patterns of behavior that have held them back or created major problems in their lives.

By understanding themselves and putting that under-standing into action, they live more authentic, productive and rewarding lives. When their behavior reflects who they *really* are, they feel a sense of integrity, a greater oneness with their soul and Spirit.

Using Dream Metaphors in Waking Life

Once we have an understanding of our own dream images, we can use these images as metaphors to bridge into other issues in our lives. Metaphors are particularly useful because they tap into our nonverbal imaging and give us a picture that symbolizes our concern.

For example, Nancy dreamed that she was playing blind man's bluff. Her associations revealed that she was avoiding a major area of emotional distress in her life. We later used the image of playing blind man's bluff to refer to her avoidance of any conflict that had a strong emotional component.

This helped her outwit an unconscious attempt to bluff her way through difficult situations where uncomfortable feelings might arise. She realized that she needed to experience her feelings and cope with them in order to move ahead. Thus, the phrase "blind man's bluff" became a metaphor in her therapy to signal avoidance.

Gary dreamed he was lost in the labyrinths of a cave high in the mountains. Everywhere he turned led to a dead end. He awoke still trapped in the cave. As we worked through his associations to the dream, he realized that the cave both trapped him and allowed him to avoid more down-to-earth issues in his life.

He realized that when he faced a difficult situation that he couldn't figure out, he would say, "I'm at a dead end." This negative metaphor ruled his life. Instead of trying a new perspective or mobilizing inner creativity, he would avoid the situation, essentially hiding out. The mountain cave dream symbolized his hideaway.

I asked Gary how he would change his mountain cave to make it a positive metaphor. He envisioned a transformational ending to his dream. He decided to keep the hideaway for strategic retreat purposes but created a secret opening to go in and out. The "dead end" metaphor became a "secret opening" metaphor. Now when he catches himself avoiding a difficult situation, he reminds himself, humorously, "Here I am, at another dead end. Where's the secret opening?" He essentially laughs at the old metaphor and figures a creative way out.

Roberta had a very disturbing dream about drowning and came to realize the dream was warning her she was overwhelmed and sinking into her unresolved emotions. Thereafter, whenever she began to feel she was "drowning," she knew it was an internal reminder to start "swimming," meaning to allow her emotions to come to the surface and to take some kind of positive, self-affirming action to tend to her own needs for comfort.

Once we train ourselves in the use of metaphor and imagery, we may find a metaphorical image flashing into our mind at the point that we need it. For example, another client, Dave, had a dream in which he and his regiment were being "called to arms," activated for duty in a war scene. This dream came at a point in his job where he had to stand up for himself under fire from his supervisor or get fired for staying silent. When Dave did stand up for himself in a firm but intelligent and diplomatic way, his supervisor was actually impressed. They worked out a solution that pleased them both.

Dave tells me that this scene has continued to flash into his mind at various points on the job when he needed to take action in a dispute. He still has a tendency to tell himself, "Just stay out of it. Don't get yourself in trouble." He laughingly says, "Each time that happens, my call-to-arms dream glyph pops up and keeps me from retiring from the battlefield when that would be exactly the wrong thing to do."

I find that people seek dream analysis for many and varied reasons. They may want to resolve symptoms or improve their mental outlook and emotional well-being. Or they may want to relate more effectively to others, to function more productively in their lives.

Above all, they want to discover their more positive and authentic self, which is hidden within. They pursue the understanding of their dreams as an avenue to an in-depth understanding of their soul and spirit.

We have explored a number of keys to the inner compartments of consciousness that hold the secrets of the soul. How can you follow through with these keys in your personal dream work?

In chapter 6, we will look more specifically at how you may help yourself remember, record and investigate your dreams. For now, I suggest you begin to keep a written record of the dreams you do remember, including your particular dream symbols and the way you tend to use metaphor in dreams and waking life.

You are a unique individual and have a special way of looking at life. Exploring and interpreting your dreams can guide you to the discovery of hidden talents, unknown virtues and better ways to create the life you want for yourself and those you love.

CHAPTER FIVE

Dreams and Visions
of Soul and Spirit

*This world is but a canvas to
our imaginations. Dreams are
the touchstones of our characters.*

—HENRY DAVID THOREAU
*A Week on the Concord
and Merrimack Rivers*

*L*et's talk a bit more about how we move into our dream life at night and what it all means at the level of our body, emotions, mind, soul and spirit.

Under normal circumstances, as we drift off to sleep our brain continues to process the problems of the day, sorting through its computer files for relevant information, facts and ideas for coping with whatever problem is uppermost in our minds. Our guardian angels and Higher Self add knowledge and instruction from higher realms, helping our minds put together various creative solutions to current difficulties.

As sleep deepens and our brain waves slow down, we enter the world of dreams. While our physical body is being restored and emotional issues processed, we may also experience mystical happenings or be instructed in higher spiritual truths.

At a soul level we learn much during sleep, although we may or may not consciously recall the instruction in the morning. Since soul experiences are often an inner knowing that is difficult to translate into words, the awareness may surface at a later time as an intuitive understanding of a certain dilemma or as having a sixth sense of how to proceed.

Guidance from the Soul

At night our soul contemplates what has happened during the day and the lessons we need to learn from it. Our soul is also processing unresolved emotional dramas or other out-of-balance states and is gauging what kind of progress we've made in pursuing our destiny.

I believe that all our dreams—whether triggered by a physical event during the night, an unresolved subconscious or unconscious situation, or a superconscious or etheric experience—are the contemplation of our soul and spirit.

No dream is unimportant. And every dream is unique to the dreamer. Even when two people dream essentially the same dream, the interpretation will differ according to each one's individual nature, thoughts and desires, karmic predicament and specific accomplishments.

Edgar Cayce, known to many as the "sleeping prophet," described the basic nature of a dream this way: "Sleep is that period when the soul takes stock of what it has acted upon from one rest period to another; drawing comparisons, as it were, that make for harmony, peace, joy, longsuffering, patience, brotherly love and kindness . . . or hate, harsh words, unkind thoughts and oppressions. The soul either abhors what it has passed through, or it enters into the joy of its Lord."[1]

While we may have various types of dreams—physical, emotional, mental, etheric, prophetic—we always benefit by analyzing a dream as a message from our soul and spirit. People sometimes question this, especially when they have what they consider a physical dream. But let's look at what may be happening when we have a physical dream.

This type of dream is usually initiated through some kind of noise or other physical experience. Thus, you may be asleep yet hear an ambulance siren wailing, a dog barking or a door slamming. Or you may experience physical discomfort from having eaten a food that distresses your body. Your husband or wife may sleepily fling an arm across your back, the curtain may blow open and brush across your face, or your puppy may jump on the bed. The temperature may change during the night so that your body gets cold or hot, or you may get thirsty or hungry in the middle of the night.

Any of these experiences might wake you up, but they may also prompt a dream that incorporates the physical happening. While you are paying little or no conscious attention to this middle-of-the-night intrusion, your soul and Higher Self incorporate your subconscious interpretation of it into a meaningful dream that allows you to process the physical disturbance and keep from waking up. It may also offer a lesson you need to learn.

We need to think twice before we discard any dream, no matter how odd or mundane it may seem. As an example, let's look at Anne's dream.

A Dreamer's Talking Horse Makes Sense

Anne, a middle-aged woman, was at home alone because her husband was on a business trip. She is fairly used to it but told me she always feels somewhat apprehensive when he's gone.

A rainstorm came during the night that aroused her briefly to sleepy wakefulness. She said to herself, "It's storming outside, but the windows are closed." Almost immediately, she fell back into a deep sleep. When she awakened again, she remembered a dream that definitely caught her attention.

As Anne described it: "I'm riding a horse on the desert when a huge lightning storm comes up. I'm worried that I'll be struck by lightning. I crouch down and head for a gully where we can get lower down. In the gully I dismount and try to get the horse to lie down. He's not interested in lying down.

"Suddenly my horse says to me, 'Don't be stupid; it's just a lightning storm.' I'm surprised the horse is talking to me and say, 'I didn't know you could talk.' He says, 'Someone around here has to keep his head.'"

Anne went on to tell me her thoughts about the dream: "The horse represents my instinctual nature, rather unpredictable at times. The desert is familiar to me. I grew up near the desert. It's kind of desolate but familiar. I don't like the idea of riding on the desert because you're too exposed to the elements. It's a long distance between places, and you can get caught in a storm or flash flood.

"The storm in my dream wreaks havoc, the same way my stormy emotions do. Lightning is scary to me. It strikes suddenly and can kill you or at least fry your brain. I can get that angry, in such a fury that I strike out unthinkingly at whatever upsets me, just like my dad. I'm actually afraid of my own anger because it can get so out of control.

"The gully in the dream is a lower place where I won't be as apt to be struck by the lightning. It's also nature's storm sewer, a channel for water when there's a storm. Metaphorically, it would keep my emotions from running all over the place. What I'm feeling in the dream is a deep fear and sense of apprehension, as if something awful is going to happen.

"The horse in the dream reminds me of a funny movie I saw about a talking horse. But I'm not laughing in the dream. I didn't appreciate being called stupid just because I didn't want to be struck by lightning. Being in the gully is like being lower down, more protected. That makes me think of getting the lowdown, getting some kind of understanding.

"I suppose I could say that horse is giving me the lowdown, even if he is being insulting. The way he said, 'Someone around here has to keep his head'—that's my husband's kind of talk when he thinks I'm getting hysterical or out of control because I'm scared about something."

What is the dreamer saying to herself? "I really was afraid of that rainstorm even though I went right back to sleep. If it hadn't bothered me, I wouldn't have dreamed about it. A childhood friend of mine was killed by a lightning strike years ago. It still upsets me when I remember it.

"Maybe that memory and the storm outside prompted the dream. That's one level of it—processing my feelings about that storm at night, my husband being away, and remembering my friend who had been killed by lightning. I'd have felt safer if my husband had been home. I always have some fear and a sense of desolation when he goes on these long trips."

"It's odd that a talking horse is the one making sense in my dream. I guess I feel two ways about my instincts, especially my anger. On the one hand I'm somewhat afraid of them because they're unpredictable. Yet I respect 'horse sense,' basic instinctual understanding.

"In the dream I'm trying to overcome fear of my basic instincts, like the unpredictability of my lightning-like anger. At the same time, I'm jesting with myself about being scared. A sense of humor is a way I try to handle things I'm scared of. Taking a humorous perspective kind of disarms the anger and dissolves the fear. It's certainly a lot better than coming unglued. I think that's what the horse, my instinctual nature, is telling me."

Anne's dream is a good example of what can be triggered by a physical happening in the night when it relates in some way to unresolved subconscious or unconscious issues.

Such dreams are typically couched in a symbolic language that needs the dreamer's associations to be fully understood. In this dream Anne's consciousness was symbolized as a desert because she grew up near a desert and because her fear and anger and the absence of her husband created a sense of desolation.

Difficult Dreams Can Be a Gift

In a relatively universal sense, we may symbolize the physical body as a house or some type of vehicle. The mind may become a form of air travel or the winging of a bird. The emotional state is reflected in the feelings we have during a dream or may appear as emotion-laden experiences—something that horrifies us, makes us angry, surprises us, disgusts us or gives us a sense of joy or inspiration.

I have also found that emotions are often represented by experiences with water, such as sitting peacefully under a waterfall, swimming in a pool, running for cover from the rain or coming close to drowning in the ocean.

Dreams from hidden compartments of consciousness bring to the surface our hopes and fears, our underlying strengths or weaknesses of character, and any self-destructive habits or undeveloped talents.

I believe such dreams come from an alliance of our outer self with our soul and spirit. Together, without the interference of our conscious defenses, we focus our attention on internal dilemmas that we need to reconcile in order to fulfill goals we have set for ourselves in life.

In our dreams, then, we dramatize our conflicting thoughts and emotions and the behaviors that get us into trouble. And we show ourselves a way out.

From deeper levels of our unconscious, we unearth hurtful and traumatic experiences that are still bothering us. These dramas can be from our current lifetime or before. When past-life happenings surface, they do so because we are ready to deal with ancient patterns that do not serve us well today.

I believe such dreams, difficult though they may be, are in reality a gift from our soul and Higher Self. They tell us it is time to learn the lessons of past experience and discover how to get beyond old dysfunctional ways. When we do this, we become alchemists in our own lives, transforming our rocky, leaden character flaws into the gold of higher aspirations.

Natalie had a repetitive dream of people being tortured. In each of these dreams, she was on a hill at a distance but close enough to see, hear and feel the terror and pain of those undergoing torture. She would awaken in a cold sweat. At one point she asked me to help her analyze the dream. She came to realize that she had been tortured in a past life and was still carrying the memory of the experience.

This remembrance also explained why she couldn't stand to watch movies that showed atrocities committed during wars or inquisitions. As she said to me, "It's like going through it myself. I can't understand why people enjoy seeing those kinds of movies. They are horrifying. And they are not the ways of God."

Natalie also realized that she was torturing herself by carrying these painful records in her unconscious mind. Thus she discovered her own inner torturer. As she brought the dream images to conscious awareness and did her spiritual and psychological work on them, they began to lessen their hold over her. Gradually they faded into nonexistence.

Although she no longer has dreams about torture, she is still very sensitive to stories of people being physically abused or tortured. As she says, "I don't think we are meant to accept those kinds of things without a sense of horror. I believe God is a being of love. He would not have us treat one another in such cruel ways. What will it take for us to wake up?"

Natalie was ready to deal with her past-life torture and therefore her soul and Higher Consciousness allowed it to surface. She worked on it with spiritual and psychological tools and is free of those dreams today.

Spiritual Protection

A friend of mine had persistent nightmares of being abducted by aliens. The nightmares began when she was a teenager. In her mid-thirties, she learned to pray to Archangel Michael so habitually and fervently that she found herself calling to him in the middle of a nightmare. From that moment on, she was never troubled by dreams of aliens again.

I remember a dream of my own a number of years ago where I awakened in the middle of the night silently screaming but uttering only a soft, strangled "help!" I had been dreaming of a huge, malevolent fiery being that was trying to capture me.

This dream became a wake-up call never to take a victim stance in the face of malevolent forces but to call upon the Lord and stand, face and confront that force. I intensified my prayers to Archangel Michael for protection and did a lot of spiritual work on the dream image through prayers and decrees.* From that time on I had no recurrence of that kind of dream.

In my spiritual studies I have learned and verified for myself that Archangel Michael is our defender in any kind of trouble, waking or sleeping. Any of us can call upon Archangel Michael for protection. Here is a simple prayer that invokes his intercession. It works for me every time.

---

*Decrees are a dynamic form of spoken prayer, used to invoke the help of angels and heavenly hosts and to direct God's light into individual, community and world conditions.

Lord Michael before,
Lord Michael behind,
Lord Michael to the right,
Lord Michael to the left,
Lord Michael above,
Lord Michael below,
Lord Michael, Lord Michael wherever I go.
I AM his love protecting here.
I AM his love protecting here.
I AM his love protecting here.[2]

Dreams from the Superconscious

In total contrast to nightmares (astral-type dreams[3]), dreams from the superconscious are visions, spiritual-retreat experiences or divine revelations that represent messages from God through our Higher Self. They also set forth our soul's higher aspirations for our life and the spiritual lessons we need to learn.

Superconscious dreams quicken our memory to the higher planes of existence. They remind us that we are spiritual beings, housed temporarily in bodies of flesh, whose eternal destiny is beyond this earthly existence. Such dreams give us the impetus to expand the narrow room of our consciousness, push through and transcend our seeming limitations, and begin to fulfill our higher vision of who we may become.

People ask me why they can wake up with uncomfortable feelings at the end of such a positive dream. Often this goes back to unresolved childhood happenings or misconceptions developed early in life.

For example, if we were brought up in the tradition of the *via dolorosa,* the sorrowful way, we might feel guilty about having happy experiences. Or if we were raised with the idea that good experiences are nearly always followed by some kind of downfall, we could awaken with a sense of foreboding.

These kinds of reactions to good dreams are in themselves potentially transformational. They allow us to become aware of wounded parts of ourselves that need to be nurtured and healed. They may also point to conscious decisions we have made that are out of alignment with the will of our Higher Self.

Using Imagery or Storytelling

When we have been stuck in a "bad" dream, one that we don't like, we can change the dream scenario or its ending once we are awake. We can use imagery, fantasy or storytelling to allow our imagination to carry us to the heights of positive resolution.

This is a useful way of empowering ourselves. We open up to the possibility of favorable change in our lives. Since it's our dream, we can reconstruct it any way we like.

For example, another client of mine, Julianne, used imagery to turn her dream into a positive reminder. In the dream she saw a large waterway with seven or eight dark battleships. One ship is charging through but doesn't crash into the others. This battleship emerges from a "mouth" between the other ships.

The dreamer is observing all this from the shoreline. She also sees a woman walking on a patch of ice and is afraid the woman will fall through. She does fall through but comes up with a smile and dry clothes.

The dreamer then turns around because she has to go back home, but now realizes she, too, will have to walk through the water. She hears herself say, "Don't walk through the deep water." As Julianne enters a state of sleepy wakefulness, she is watching children dancing through the water and follows them. In her reverie, she, too, comes out totally dry and says to herself, "It won't be so bad."

In the dream we can see that Julianne is scared of deep water, the depths of her troubles, and that she feels a sense of imminent disaster, whether through the battleships or the woman falling into the water. The woman coming up dry begins a turnaround of her feelings.

She sees she is worrying about a disaster that doesn't turn out to be one. Yet she gets upset again when she realizes she is going to have to walk through the water to get home. At this point she begins to wake herself up and, in a semi-reverie state, creates a happy ending. Her innocent, playful, trusting, child-like nature dances through the water and she follows suit.

As Julianne associates to this dream and her waking reverie, she realizes that in order to come out of deep waters dry, she needs to integrate with her childlike consciousness—her original state of innocence, an inner tranquility also apparent in the woman who came out dry.

Her statement reminded us both of Jesus' words, "Suffer the little children to come unto me, and forbid them not: for of such is the kingdom of God. Verily I say unto you, Whosoever shall not receive the kingdom of God as a little child, he shall not enter therein."[4]

Julianne's dream message? "I need to let go of my fears and emotional conflicts. And I do that by claiming my spiritual sensitivity and my playful, trusting, childlike nature. Then I can dance through my troubles instead of drowning in them."

Julianne wanted to remind herself not to give in to her warring part that is the antithesis of her soul's childlike nature. So she used imagery and drew a diagram of the battleship scene. She put a person's mouth right in the middle of it to remind herself of the emotional warfare that can come out through words.

Hints about Handling Our Lives

All of us can benefit from creating a visual illustration of an important dream, as Julianne did with her battleship diagram. We can also develop rituals that reinforce our dream message and the changes we want to anchor because of it.

For instance, if we have a difficult dream that ends in a beautiful natural setting, we might make it a habit of going for a walk when we feel stressed. If a dream reveals a creative way of handling a sticky issue, we might give it a try the next time a similar issue comes up.

We can take hints from our dreams about all sorts of things—decorating our homes, relating to one another more lovingly and constructively, or trying a creative approach to old problems.

Many times our dreams directly suggest some type of

training or course of study, such as taking a workshop on conflict resolution, learning how to play an instrument or taking a course in music appreciation. Sometimes our dreams tell us it's time to do spiritual work on a particular dilemma we are having difficulty resolving. The dream may even specify the type of spiritual work to do, such as meditation, visualization, prayers, decrees or mantras.

Sometimes a superconscious dream is a healing dream. We might experience the healing touch of an angel, be given a healing herb or enfolded in a special healing light. Such dreams often mark a turning point in an illness. At other times we may be given a diagnosis of a physical problem or instruction about a remedy to follow. Edgar Cayce, for example, brought forth from the inner world many physical remedies for those who sought his help.

Cayce had a unique dream concerning an infirmity in his own body. In the dream, the part of the body that needed healing was symbolized as a wheel in his brain. He called it a "dream of being crazy and of looking into my head and fixing a wheel that had stopped running, owing to a particle of dirt or trash getting into it."

He interpreted the dream as telling him "the eliminations are poor in the system" and that this was affecting his brain. He described it as "a purely physical condition" to be remedied by being "oiled up, or lubricated—that the drosses [impurities] may be removed from the physical body... so that the brain may function normally."[5]

Elsie Sechrist reports several other of Cayce's dream

interpretations concerning the health of the body. In one such interpretation, "a woman who dreamed she was entering Mexico illegally to buy chocolates was merely reminding herself in sleep that she had been warned against eating chocolate. The 'illegal entry into Mexico' symbolized her abuse of the laws of health. Mexico was associated by her with the illegal transportation of narcotics injurious to the body."

This same woman had another warning when "she dreamed she had been presented with a rolled document with the word 'Will' printed on it. Believing it to be an important inheritance, she unrolled the paper and read the single word 'Chocolate.' Why did the dream refer her to the will? Because willpower is the gift of God to man, and she was not using it properly in relationship to chocolate."[6]

Sechrist tells of another dreamer who saw a skull and crossbones on a cup of coffee. "Upon questioning her, she admitted to drinking fifteen to twenty cups of coffee per day. Presumably the dream was informing her that she was poisoning herself through excessive assimilation of caffeine. She took the suggestion and cut down to six cups per day."[7]

Messages from the Heaven World

Messages from the heaven world may come when we are fully awake, especially during devotional experiences. They may also happen when we are halfway between sleeping and waking, or during deeper levels of sleep where we dream. When we receive such a message, we are left with a profound sense of awe and gratitude.

Such occurrences remind us of the biblical account of the calling of Samuel to God's service as a prophet:

> And the child Samuel ministered unto the Lord before Eli. And the word of the Lord was precious in those days; there was no open vision. And it came to pass at that time, when Eli was laid down in his place, and his eyes began to wax dim, that he could not see. And ere the lamp of God went out in the temple of the Lord, where the ark of God was, and Samuel was laid down to sleep, that the Lord called Samuel. And he answered, Here am I. And he ran unto Eli, and said, Here am I, for thou calledst me. And he said, I called not; lie down again.
>
> And he went and lay down. And the Lord called yet again, Samuel. And Samuel arose and went to Eli, and said, Here am I, for thou didst call me. And he answered, I called not, my son; lie down again. Now Samuel did not yet know the Lord, neither was the word of the Lord yet revealed unto him. And the Lord called Samuel again the third time. And he arose and went to Eli, and said, Here am I, for thou didst call me. And Eli perceived that the Lord had called the child.
>
> Therefore Eli said unto Samuel, Go, lie down. And it shall be, if he call thee, that thou shalt say, Speak, Lord, for thy servant heareth. So Samuel went and lay down in his place. And the Lord came, and stood, and called as at other times, Samuel, Samuel. Then Samuel answered, Speak, for thy servant heareth.[8]

Thus God spoke to the child Samuel as he slept and called him to service as his prophet.

Author Ann Spangler reminds us of the dream Saint Francis of Assisi had when he was a young soldier on his way to war: "In his dream, he saw a magnificent array of shields, spears, and armor. Then he heard a voice saying, 'All this shall belong to you and your warriors.' At first he mistook the dream for a prediction of distinction in battle. Only later did he recognize it as a prophetic picture of the thousands who would follow his example, becoming spiritual soldiers in the service of the Gospel."[9]

Spangler also reminds us that the biblical Gideon won his remarkable victory partly as a result of a dream interpretation. "Gideon overheard an enemy recount a dream to a fellow soldier, predicting that Gideon's army would rout their own. The soldier had dreamed of a round loaf of barley bread that tumbled into camp and struck the tent with such force that it collapsed. After listening to the dream, the second warrior replied, 'This can be nothing other than the sword of Gideon. God has given us into his hands.' Hearing the dream recounted and its interpretation gave Gideon courage, and he and his men won a remarkable victory."[10]

People of many different spiritual traditions value certain dreams and visions as guidance messages. It is accepted in Islam that God can speak to men and women in the form of such visions when a person is asleep or in a state of meditation. The Book of Revelation in the Bible is the vision of the apostle John on the island of Patmos, where he had been exiled. As we have seen, people of India, China and the ancient Israelites, Egyptians and Greeks all prized what they considered to be divine messages in their dreams.

Visions may be a calling from God to our soul, as were the visions of Bernadette Soubirous of Lourdes, France. Bernadette's visions of the Virgin Mary occurred in 1858. She was gathering firewood along the Gave River when she heard a sound like thunder coming from a grotto. When she investigated it, she saw the Virgin.

Our Lady appeared to Bernadette eighteen times over the next few months. After one of the apparitions, a spring began to flow in the grotto exactly where the Lady said it would. It has continued to flow with healing powers ever since, and Lourdes has become a pilgrimage center for Christianity, a place of miracles to many who have sought healing. In 1933 Pope Pius XI officially recognized Bernadette as a saint.

I believe that superconscious dreams and heavenly visions come from God as divine guideposts. Their messages aid us in our spiritual journey or perhaps warn us of dangers along the way. Such mystical experiences signify the soul's higher state of consciousness—that the soul has access to higher spiritual planes as well as a willingness to seek and accept divine direction.

Dreams and visions may thus bring to the conscious mind matters of vital importance to the soul. They may convey instruction from angels or masters and reveal various aspects of the soul's purpose. If we ask for divine guidance, prepare ourselves spiritually through prayer and meditation, and practice eternal principles in our daily living, we may receive such experiences.

How to Recognize Past-Life Clues in a Dream

At times we receive dream messages from our soul that indicate past-life experiences. The more dreams we record, the more clues we receive about these past lives. And the more understanding we have about the past lives, the better we understand the meaning of circumstances in our lives today.

How, then, do we recognize a dream that gives us clues from a past life? You may find yourself dressed in clothing from a different period of history or using tools or weapons that seem to date from a different place and time. If you dream you are dressed in the style of the French Revolution, for example, or that you are a sailor on a Roman galley ship or are grinding corn with a rock and pestle, the odds are that your dream contains clues to a past life.

Sometimes you may recognize a figure from history in a past-life dream. You may or may not have been that person, but there is something about him or her and the meaning of that one's life that connects with your life at that time. Write the story of the dream, give the dream a name and write down the lesson for the soul as you understand it.

Meditate upon what seems to be the past-life detail or theme. Ask your Higher Self to help you tune into whatever is important for your soul to know or remember. Focus your mind on it. Visualize the scene, the image, the person, and let it expand and move and become more detailed. Allow your imagery to carry you through to some kind of resolution or stopping point. Then write down what you remember from your active meditation. At times an entire past-life recall may come to you in this way.

Look back through your dream journal for other dreams that have a similar lesson, challenge or resolution. You may find a theme that clues you in to an important shift you need to make, either in your consciousness or your way of handling your life today.

Ask yourself, "Is anything in this dream similar to something happening to me now?" If so, meditate upon the possible connection and what you were meant to learn from this past life. Ask yourself, "How does it connect with my lessons in this life?" Ask the angels to help you understand.

Remember, your soul is always trying to learn and grow, to become more of who God ordained you to be, to be restored by grace, to arrive once more in the higher octaves of light, to celebrate the soul's eternal destiny, reunion with God.

CHAPTER SIX

Creating Your Dream Journal

Dreams are faithful interpreters of our inclinations; but there is art required to sort and understand them.

—MICHEL DE MONTAIGNE
"Of Experience"

*I*f we look back through history, we see that leaders of the people have experienced dreams, visions or visitations from higher realms. These have heralded the destiny of individuals or guided the fortunes of cultures and nations.

We, too, may choose to listen to the voice of God or the angels and understand and live our dreams.

Your Destiny and Life Mission

Even as the world's adepts and spiritual mentors received divine guidance through dreams and visions, they taught their followers that they too could walk the path of fulfilling their soul's destiny.

I believe all of us have our own heroic path to walk. All of us have a special gift to offer to Earth and the children of Earth. No one else can offer your gift in quite the same way as you. It is your special blessing to pass on to others.

Each of us has a chapter of divine destiny to write and fulfill. We can pursue that destiny through living our sense of the heaven world while we are on Earth. This means different things to different people, which can result in a rich admixture of blessings throughout the earth. I believe it is always possible to fulfill benevolent hopes and dreams in our own sphere of influence.

Edgar Cayce once stated, "Dreams guide and help us after we set our goals and ideals for our lives."[1] This is wise counsel for us today.

I suggest that you focus on what you really value, that you cultivate your particular talents and that you pursue your higher desires. As you do so, you may receive a vision, a guidance dream, an insight about a special calling or a glimpse of divine direction for your life mission.

You can also have a sense of mission whether or not you have a specific guidance experience. Perhaps that mission is reflected in your natural talents, your favorite activities, your daydreams of what you would like your life to become. Look at these possibilities, these potential directions, and set about making your inner hopes and wishes come true.

Once you have a vision or a sense of direction, give some thought to setting specific goals. Meeting those goals can become your personal measuring rod of progress. By defining your short-term and long-term goals, you are on your way to keying into your life mission. This is important because your mission, or *dharma* as Eastern traditions teach it, is a part of the initiatic path* that helps your soul fulfill her divine destiny on Earth.

Ask for a Guidance Dream or Vision

If a clear picture of your soul's destiny eludes you, pray, meditate and ask your Higher Self and guardian angels to

---

*The initiatic path refers to the strait gate and narrow way that leadeth unto Life (Matt. 7:14). It is the path whereby the disciple seeks to overcome, step-by-step, the limitations of selfhood in time and space and attain reunion with the Infinite One.

reveal it to you. As you focus and ask for guidance in this way, you set the stage for an inner knowing, a higher vision or a guidance dream. And remember, when you call for divine direction, don't hang up before you hear the answer. Keep that inner connection open.

You might ask yourself right now, "What are my hopes and dreams? What are my gifts and talents? How do they suggest a direction that may connect with my mission in life, with my soul's destiny?" You might draw a picture or write a brief description of what comes to mind. Stay open to the inner promptings of your soul and Higher Self. Allow your vision and understanding to expand as more awareness comes to you.

When you have a sense of your mission and are committed to achieving specific goals, your determination and focus will draw to you a flow of ideas, opportunities and the general wherewithal to accomplish what you have envisioned. You will be amazed at how doors will open, help will materialize and the needed strength, tools and financial support will appear out of nowhere.

Remember, higher vision needs to be coupled with right motivation, positive attitude, emotional mastery and constructive action. Cultivating a wise and compassionate approach will help you move forward in a way that is congruent with your soul's hopes and dreams. Such self-mastery provides a firm foundation for success in your life mission.

Starting a Dream Journal

I suggest that you start a dream journal in which you record your dreams and your understanding of them. It is much more useful to keep a journal than to jot down your dreams on scraps of paper here and there. As you record your dreams in a journal, you will begin to see parallels and themes.

As preparation for your dream work you may wish to reflect on the following questions. They may help draw out the threads of your soul's aspirations and concerns. Jot down whatever thoughts come to mind as you ask yourself the following questions:

- Who are my heroes and heroines?

- What are the principles and ideals I try to live by?

- What do I want to accomplish in life?

- What is my highest vision of my soul's destiny fulfilled?

- How does my soul's mission on Earth connect with my childhood dreams, youthful aspirations and adult choices?

- What do I need to do right now to start making my dreams come true?

- Do I feel good about my physical body, my emotions and desires, my personal habits, my home life, my use of free time, my spiritual life?

- What can I do to take more loving care of myself? What changes in my personal lifestyle would feel good to me?

- What goals do I want to set for this year, this month, this week?

- What actions do I need to take to meet my goals?

- How am I going to motivate myself?

- When I look back on my life, what do I want to have accomplished for myself, my soul, my loved ones and the family of Earth?

Keep these questions and the notes you have made of your answers in the back of your dream journal so that you can refer to them as you do your dream work.

Chart Your Major Life Experiences

I suggest that you begin dream journaling with a written review of your personal history. Record the major happenings of your life from birth up to the present time. Include such things as physical events, emotional happenings, intellectual achievements, family, school and work experiences, special activities, dreams, unusual or notable events, spiritual highlights, soul lessons or anything else you consider to be important.

You might even want to make this a separate journal, your life journal. You can continue to record meaningful events and experiences as the months and years roll by and correlate them with the entries in your dream journal.

Chart the events chronologically from birth. List each year on a separate page or pages, especially if you have a number of major events to record. Leave several blank pages after each year.

You will find those pages useful for recording other memories as they come to mind or for adding events that friends or family may remember. Who knows? One day you might want to write your memoirs as a book to be cherished by family and friends. You will already have all the memories in one place.

Start with anything you know about your birth circumstances and major events that occurred in that first year. Add any commentary that comes to mind. Skip some pages. Begin your next entry with anything of importance that happened between the ages of one and two. Add your thoughts about those events. Keep recording your memories, year by year, noting and commenting on these events of your life.

When you are finished, write a brief summary of the threads you see running through your experiences. Place this summary in your dream journal as a point of reference to help you connect your dreams to your waking life.

Remembering and Recording Your Dreams

Now that you have your life experiences as a point of reference, you have set the stage to begin recording your dreams. Ask God to illumine you through your dreams. As you begin to remember and record your dreams, look for themes, especially those that repeat themselves. Gradually you will begin to see a thread of higher meaning in your dreams and discern the guiding presence of your Higher Self and your guardian angels.

Gayle Delaney, author of *Living Your Dreams* and *All about Dreams,* suggests the following simple steps to help remember and record your dreams. I use them myself and recommend them highly:

1. Keep a pen and paper at your bedside.

2. Get enough sleep. Most of us need eight or more hours to feel our best and recall our dreams easily. If you need an alarm to wake you or a cup of coffee to feel good in the morning, you probably are not getting enough sleep.

3. Before sleep, write out your day notes in your journal—just four lines about what you did and felt that day. This will greatly increase your recall in the morning.

4. Wake up naturally. This way, you will usually awaken right after your longest dream of the night.

5. Lie still for a moment and learn to ask yourself, "What was just going through my mind?" Form the habit of thinking this thought before you ask yourself what day it is or what you have to do today.

6. Take your time and write out your dream as you remember it. If you are rushed, jot down a few notes. They may suffice to bring back the dream when you have more time.

7. If you don't remember a dream, force yourself to write one sentence about whatever you were feeling or whatever first came into your mind as you awoke.

8. If you start remembering too many dreams, decide how many you want to recall and how many you want to record. One dream a week is plenty if you interview yourself and learn from it.[2]

Each time you record a dream, give it a title and enter the date and time. Write down how you felt during the dream and when you awakened, and then write the dream's overall theme and detailed content.

Once you have recorded a dream, the next step is to free-associate to each image and reflect on the overall picture that emerges. As you do this, you gain insight into the meaning of the dream.

As the last step, ask yourself, "What is the dream message? How does it apply to my life? What specific actions do I want to take?"

Refer to your life journal as you record and analyze your dreams. Look for points of connection between the dream and your life experiences. You may also find yourself remembering an earlier dream. See how it relates to a current one or to past or present-day experiences. It's a good idea to leave a few pages between each dream entry to allow space to note the connections with subsequent dreams or your flashes of insight.

As you increasingly understand the symbolism of your dream images and the connection to your waking life, you more and more get a sense of your major life issues—and the major dramas of your soul. You also begin to get a perspective on lessons learned and others still to be mastered.

Sometimes people do not have the time or inclination to record their dreams during the week. If this is the case for you, simply become a weekend dreamer. Ask the angels and your Higher Self to help you remember important dreams on the weekends, and make it a point to record and interpret them.

Remember to keep your dream journal and a flashlight or lighted pen right beside your bed so that you can write the dream down as soon as you awaken. If you let time go by before recording a dream, you will likely lose much of its content as it recedes into the superconscious, subconscious or unconscious realm from which it came.

Analyzing and Learning from Your Dreams

Here is an outline to help you analyze your dreams after you have recorded them. My clients find it a good way to organize their dream impressions.

- Title, date and time of dream.

- How I felt during the dream, and how I felt when I awakened.

- Detailed description of the dream, including the people, setting, conversations, actions, etc. What parts of the dream stand out the most?

- What is the major theme of this dream? What associations, thoughts, memories and feelings does it trigger in me?

- What is the background context of my dream? What is happening in my life at this time?

- Who are the people that I recognize in my dream and what are their outstanding characteristics, both in the dream and as I know them in real life? Which part of me is each person playing?

- Who are the other people in my dream? What are their outstanding characteristics? Which parts of me are these people playing?

- What part of me is symbolically represented in the dream's setting (house, office, nature scene, busy street, flood, fire, etc.)? What parts of me are symbolized by the various objects or animals in the dream (car, boat, motorcycle, airplane, grass, trees, buildings, factory, fish, horses, cows, etc.)?

- What is the dream's message for me? What is the lesson my soul is trying to learn?

- How will I apply what I have learned from this dream in my life?

Periodically, ask yourself the following questions and jot down the answers that come to mind in a special place in your journal. Refer to it once a week.

- What are my visions and dreams telling me about my spiritual goals? How am I doing? Am I achieving my goals? Am I nurturing my soul? How?

- What are my personal goals, including physical, emotional and mental well-being? What are my goals for home, career, relationships and leisure activities? How am I doing in defining and pursuing my mission?

- What guidance am I getting through my intuition and my Higher Self? What studies and daily practices will help me respond to that guidance?

As we periodically review our goals, we may also find it helpful to ask ourselves, "What are my dreams telling me about the needs of my soul? What are my spiritual values, the character qualities that are of intrinsic worth to me? What are my principles, the inner code of conduct that guides my actions? Am I practicing these principles in my daily life?"

Take a few moments to reflect and redirect yourself accordingly. For example, if one of your higher values is "soul integrity," the associated principle might be "I will be true to myself and to my God in my words and actions." You might then ask yourself, "How have I been true to myself and my God in my words and actions today?"

One final thought—be sure to address your dream material in your prayers and meditations. I suggest giving the "I AM Light" and violet-flame mantras* for the transmutation of any negative images, thoughts and feelings. Then create a new vision for yourself by invoking specific positive images, thoughts and feelings to take their place.

Ask your Higher Self and the angels for the divine antidote to your problems. Call for the divine matrix of your soul's purpose in life and the vision of it to descend into your conscious awareness. Set the new vision in your consciousness through the use of I AM affirmations. Now, you can put it all into action.

Create Your Own Dream Dictionary

Classical dream symbolism has been the subject of many books and dream dictionaries. At times it may be useful to

*See pages 127, 128, 129.

consult a dream dictionary just to get an idea of how certain symbols were interpreted in different cultures.[3]

However, as we have seen, dream symbols are used uniquely by the individual dreamer. You have your own way of metaphorically symbolizing the ups and downs of your life and the dramas of your soul. You have your own culture, your own inner world, where the secrets of your soul are to be explored and revealed.

How about creating your own dream dictionary? As you identify common symbols in your dreams, you are learning your own metaphorical language and how it expresses your inner values, motivations, memories, thoughts, feelings and physical habits.

Every time you realize how you symbolize a certain aspect of your feelings or motivations, put it in your dictionary. A good system is to list each symbol and then record its personal meaning from your dreams.

And remember that each dream is meant to convey a particular message from your soul and Higher Self. That message may be many-faceted, but it always implies action that moves you forward on your journey in life.

Reset the Program and Live Your Dreams

As we have seen, our dreams show us inner patterns in our lives. They also show us the problems and events of the day or what we anticipate tomorrow. All of this is in the light of our sense of inner purpose and vision and the goals we have set for ourselves.

Much of this, however, operates at a subconscious or unconscious level. At those levels, we retain old beliefs and habits. Our lives are run by this old programming until we replace it.

If we have not reset our inner programming, we may still be caught up in trying to please our parents or in vying with brothers and sisters for their attention. We may find ourselves acting from the old programming in our present family life or in our career, our social life, or even our spiritual endeavors.

How do we reset the program? How do we live our dreams?

First of all, we need to have a sense of what our life is all about—spiritually, mentally, emotionally and physically.

At the spiritual level, we need to know that our soul has a divine destiny and a specific mission for this lifetime. We know this, of course, at inner levels, but we need to bring it to outer awareness. We do this by paying attention to our dreams, our visions and our meditations, for our soul reveals her sense of destiny in these more subtle practices.

We can decide to take our dreams seriously and set about making the good dreams come true. We can ask God to help us understand our life's mission.

We may come to understand even more about our mission in retrospect—by looking back at various choices we have made and the results of our actions or inactions. Once we understand the implications of our past choices, we can focus on the lessons learned and apply them to decisions we make today.

During the night, with the help of angels, ascended beings

and our Higher Self, we assess how we are doing. We set each new course of our waking life accordingly. This entire process of self-analysis, insight and interior correction gradually resets the inner dial of our consciousness to reflect the true desires of our soul. Ultimately, we find to our joy that the dreams of our soul have become a way of life.

Through constructive daytime activities and nightly journeys to the realms of light, each one of us pursues the fulfillment of our soul's life purpose. As we explore the secrets of our soul, we catch a glimpse of our eternal destiny.

Dream Journaling

Preparation

1. Get an attractive notebook or diary that you use only for dream journaling.

2. Keep your dream journal and pen or a tape recorder by your bedside. (A lighted pen or night light is helpful so you don't have to turn on the light when you wake up during the night.)

3. As you are winding down, notice what you are thinking about or reflecting on from the daytime happenings. Make a few notes in your journal about your day and your mood upon retiring.

4. Before sleep, meditate, pray or give spiritual mantras. Ask the angels and your Higher Self to help you remember your dreams.

Upon Awakening

1. Whenever you awaken, lie still and ask yourself, "What am I dreaming about?" Write down everything that comes to mind (people, objects, setting, conversations, actions, etc.).

2. Ask yourself, "What am I feeling?" Write down your emotions in the dream and your mood upon awakening.

3. "What parts of the dream stand out the most for me?" Make a note in your journal.

4. "What seems nonsensical or irrelevant?" Jot it down.

Free-Associating

1. Ask yourself, "When have I had the same emotions or mood in my waking life as I experienced in the dream?" Write down everything that comes to mind.

2. "What seems to be the major theme of this dream?" Write it down.

3. "What memories or thoughts does this theme trigger in me?" Record these associations.

4. "Who are the people that I recognize in my dream? What are their outstanding characteristics, both in the dream and as I know them in real life? Which part of me is each person playing?" Write all of this down.

5. "Who are the other people in my dream? What are their characteristics? Which parts of me are these other people playing?" Record your responses.

6. "What part of me is symbolically represented by the dream's setting (house, office, temple, nature scene, city)? Or circumstance (stranded in the desert, flying in an airplane, swimming in a pool, running away from danger, listening to a message from an angel or master)?" Write it down.

7. "What parts of me are symbolized by various objects (car, furniture, clothing, gems, tools)? Or animals (pets, birds and bees, whales, horses, lions, bears)?" Write your associations.

8. Summarize everything you have learned by giving your dream a title (also record the date and time).

Gaining Insight

1. Pretend you are the playwright (which you really are). Ask yourself, "What was my intention in creating this dream drama?" Write a brief explanation.

2. As the dreamer, ask, "What is my dream message?" Describe its essence in a few words. Or express it in a drawing.

3. Now ask yourself, "How does the dream message relate to my daily life?"

4. "What spiritual lesson is my soul trying to learn?"

Applying the Dream Message in Your Life

1. Ask yourself, "How can I apply what I have learned in my daily life? What new habits would outwit and replace the old, negative ones?" (You may find creative visualization or guided imagery useful in this process.)

2. It is very helpful to address your dream material in prayers, mantras, decrees or meditations. By focusing on spiritual concepts and invoking light (spiritual energy) through the creative power of sound, you can transmute and transform the uncomfortable aspects of your dreams.

3. Claim your transformational victories! They are foundational to putting on "higher consciousness" in your daily life.

Creating Your Own Dream Dictionary

1. You may want to create your personal dream dictionary. I suggest a separate attractive notebook for this purpose.

2. Every time you understand how you symbolize a certain aspect of your attitudes, thoughts, feelings or habit patterns, put the symbol in your dream dictionary.

3. List each symbol or metaphor separately, followed by its personal meaning in your dreams.

4. You may discover that a particular symbol or metaphor has more than one meaning to you. For example, water may usually symbolize your emotions, but in a particular case swimming through water might be a metaphor for "going with the flow." In that case, you may want to cross-reference the two different meanings: "water" and "swimming through water."

5. As you develop your dream dictionary, you will find it useful for reference in analyzing your dreams. It is very rewarding to understand your own soul's personal use of symbols and metaphor. I suggest, however, that you continue the free-associating process because your creative soul may come up with new associations.*

---

*I have created this *Dream Journaling* section for you to use in your dream work. You are welcome to photocopy these pages for your personal use.

CHAPTER SEVEN

Discoveries from the Land of Shadows

When the gray stranger shows up in
your dream ... You know that if you
were for a time in mortal danger, and
are so still, it was not from a stranger.

—HOWARD NEMEROV
Nightmare

What about shadow or astral dreams that are extremely unpleasant, verging on a nightmare quality? Everything in this kind of dream is also a part of who we are, but we often do not recognize the shadow parts of ourselves because they seem so scary.

While such dreams are symbolic, they are also concretely applicable to our lives. The symbolism is known to the soul even when it is confusing or frightening to the outer mind. The fact that the outer mind is confused or frightened by a dream indicates that we may be shrinking from a lesson we need to learn in our waking life.

Shadow dreams may also be an expression of underlying fears, desires or records of trauma that we haven't faced or resolved. We may have decided, subconsciously, that these experiences are best dealt with in a dream, so that the memory of them will not suddenly pop up at the wrong time—interrupting us in the middle of work or as we interact with other people.

Transformation through a Poisonous Snake Dream

I remember such a shadow dream reported by a lovely older woman, Alicia. She dreamed that a long snake had gone down her throat. She thought it was poisonous and began pulling it out. She said to herself, "Oh, yes, there's the head. I got it all out." She awoke feeling a bit shaky but proud of herself.

I asked Alicia, "What does a poisonous snake mean to you?"

She replied with a slight shudder, "A poisonous snake is slithery, sneaky, quick moving. The head is where the venom comes out through the mouth. *Poisonous* means something that kills you when you swallow it. It's quick-moving poison, which makes me think of those lethal put-downs from my ex-husband. Even though I knew it was his stuff, I took it in. It's like I swallowed it and reacted inside of myself. I'd get hurt, frustrated, oversensitive and angry, but I didn't express it much.

"It's the same reaction I had to my mother, who was extremely controlling. I don't like being controlled. I get confused and lose my center when I'm around others with strong opinions. It's as though I take in other people's negative opinions, like the snake's poison. Then I put myself down the same way. I know that putting myself down is a block between my Higher Self and me. In the dream, I am removing that block. That feels pretty good."

"Yes, it's great, isn't it?" I responded. "How would you phrase your dream message?"

Alicia thought for a minute or so and replied, "I am freeing myself from poisonous thoughts, feelings and words—put-downs that have been killing me. I forgive those who have hurt me. I invoke God's light to transmute all hurt and negative thinking. I claim my right to be who I am. This is actually a transforming dream for me." She liked her response so much that she wrote it all down.

Consciously understanding the meaning of such a dream helps us face and resolve the fears, traumas and untoward desires that are holding us back from our higher quest. The dream acts as a warning, telling us we need to clean up our act, so to speak. We need to change our negative patterns that relate to the dream's images. Or perhaps we need to change our equally negative reaction to those patterns when they surface in someone else.

A Recurring Shadow Dream: Mirrors and Variations on a Theme

We all occasionally have bad dreams. They are often a combination of our own negative energy and other people's energy that we have taken in. They may also be the arcing of attention back and forth between us. Thus, energy from someone who is focusing attention upon us can enter our world and our dreams. When the energy is so influential that we are dreaming about it, we need to own it on a temporary basis so that we can let it go.

Grace, an old friend of mine who is very serious about her spiritual path, had a dream that illustrates this kind of interchange of energies. She described it, "My husband and I are in a car and this woman who has in real life chased after him for years comes up to us. She's pleasant, and in the dream I'm surprised that she isn't angry with me since I'm with my husband.

"Later in the dream I find out that he has been calling her once a week out of sympathy, feeling sorry for her. And when my back is turned and she is looking into the car, he is whispering that he loves her. I find out about all of this and get very angry. I tell him, 'It's over. Don't go back to her.'"

Grace told me that this is a recurring dream that has happened over and over with very slight variations on the theme. In the dream her husband always gets sympathetic with this woman and Grace gets very angry and tells him, "It's over. And don't go back to her."

In the particular dream she was sharing with me, after she tells him, "It's over," Stan, her husband, is sitting slumped down and looking very emasculated. She changes her mind and approaches him instead of walking away, her usual reaction. She feels compassion for him. She tells him that she will forgive him and they can try to work it out if he will go to this woman, tell her it's over, that he doesn't love her and that he will never see her again.

Grace described her husband as he appeared in this dream: "Stan is being deceptive, telling this woman who's chasing him that he loves her when he actually doesn't. He just feels sorry for her. He's also being deceptive to me, trying to make me think there's nothing going on. He's being totally controlled by his reactions to me and to her. It's actually the same way I feel when I get angry—I'm out of control and my energy drains out of me."

I asked, "What about the woman in the dream?"

Grace responded, "She's like an archetype of a fallen woman—glamorous, passive, sympathetic and on the make. She represents the archetypal seductive female who is superficial and empty inside. She feeds off of other people. She's just like my mom and like some other women, so-called friends, in my life. They live on the surface. As long as you admire them and do everything they want, they're nice to you. When you have to confront them about something, they get angry and either ignore you or turn on you.

"My mom is just like the woman who goes after my husband—the same archetypal sympathetic, glamorous, beautiful, seductive, rich woman. They both represent my shadow passions, ways I used to behave when I was young, before I had awakened to my spiritual path. I never liked being that way though. It wasn't who I really am."

I asked about her emotions, "What does it mean to you that you get so angry in the dream?"

She said with a sigh, "That's a side of me I'm still trying to change. I realize it's my angry shadow side. I flip from being passive and sympathetic, like this woman in the dream, to getting angry. Stan does the same thing. We're mirrors for each other when it comes to the sympathetic and then angry reactions."

In her associations Grace thought of another related dream: "I have another recurring dream about a man I was once involved with who took advantage of me. When I dream about this other man, he is always trying to convince me that he has changed, and in the dream he does all the right things. He wants me to marry him. I want to believe him, but I'm not convinced that he has changed. I can't remember an ending where it becomes clear one way or the other."

I asked her, "What do you think you are telling yourself through this dream?"

She responded, "This man I was once involved with represents the fallen masculine side of me [the negative animus]. He is attractive, rich, and trying to seduce me. He gets angry when he doesn't get what he wants. He's like my dad, charming but very angry. He's the masculine version of the woman who's chasing after my husband in the first dream."

As we discussed her dreams, the following picture emerged: Grace and Stan believe they are twin flames, twin souls. This means they were created by God at the same time and have identical patterns at the level of the divine, like twin suns. Once on Earth, they got separated because they fell prey to people like the ones she dreams about.

As twin flames, Grace and Stan have a very close connection, even when they are not together. They can feel each other's feelings and mirror each other's responses to life. When they get into relationships with people who betray them, they absorb that negative energy and consciousness. Since they are so close, they pass the energy and consciousness back and forth between them until they finally recognize what is going on. Then they do spiritual work together to transform the energy they have taken in and to heal their relationship.

The Role of the Shadow and the Animus in Our Lives

Grace realized that the theme in her dreams—of getting sympathetically involved with people who later turn around and betray them—also has been playing out in their business interactions. She and Stan get sympathetic and want to help someone out, so they go into a business deal with that person. Then the inevitable letdown comes when the person betrays them.

This drama also shows itself in other business relationships. For example, two of Stan's business associates have the same kind of controlling anger as Grace's father and the man in her second dream who appears as the seducer (the negative animus).

Grace also talked about her husband at one time having to report to a dominating woman who was in charge of everything. This woman was another kind of fallen woman archetype, one whose negative-animus power trips and bossy, tyrannical, angry behavior made everyone miserable in the work situation. She is like the flip side of the sympathetic, seductive, shadow woman who is chasing Stan in the first dream. That woman appears passive but is tyrannical underneath.

Whenever we have a close connection with another person, we tend to absorb his or her attitudes, mind-sets, emotions and ways of behaving. Psychologically, we call what we take in from others "introjects." Thus twin souls carry one another's introjects, meaning they share whatever they have taken in from people, including those who have lured and betrayed them.

In the case of my friend and her husband, their mutual underlying shadow theme is that of sympathizing with the troubles of rich and beautiful people and getting angry when those people betray their trust.

How do we deal with this kind of situation that is

happening in a dream and in real life? First, we need to understand our conscious thoughts and feelings, then our negative shadow side and the dynamics of our animus or anima as they appear in the dream.[1]

Next, we can do the psychological and spiritual work to transform negative potentials indicated in the dream—negative attitudes, thoughts, feelings and habits. Then, we can choose to replace these negatives with a positive matrix that upholds the integrity of the person we want to be.

Finally, we can mobilize the necessary positive energy to get beyond the drama and move on. All of this takes effort and determination, but it's worth it.

In the case of Grace's dreams, her transformational work is first to recognize her negative shadow, the angry feminine side of herself, and then begin to transform it. How? By not allowing its usual angry expression. That means she needs to claim her inner power by standing up for herself in a calm manner and expressing herself as the intuitive, wise, loving woman she really is.

Transforming the Shadow Self

Grace's transformational process of her shadow self has four key steps, each of which requires effort on her part.

The first step is to consciously surrender her major negative shadow pattern (the anger) and claim a positive replacement for it. Grace is already doing this. She is changing the drama at an energetic level by invoking God's light and love through her decrees, mantras and affirmations.

The next step is to change the mind-set that usually provokes the anger. Rather than moving into a victim stance or vengeful thinking, Grace is praying for guidance and following her spiritual intuition. She is also practicing a positive attitude toward solving the problem. She recognizes that no matter what the circumstances are, the anger is an issue of her own soul.

The third step is to recognize the early signs of anger, refuse to act on it and exchange the anger for compassionate understanding toward herself and her husband. After all, they are in the same boat. They both need to take charge of their unruly passions and transform them into love and compassion for one another.

The last step is to practice standing up for herself in a calm, firm and loving way.

Grace is taking these steps, and it is working. She and her husband have made a pact to help each other transform their shadow sides, and they are more in love than ever.

This last occurrence of the dream with her husband demonstrates that Grace is making progress on the entire drama, even at the unconscious level. Instead of avoiding the encounter by walking away (the shadow victim) or reacting angrily (the shadow aggressor), she faces her negative animus. Compassionately she offers him an opportunity to handle the situation in a forthright way. As she does so, she feels better about herself and becomes the director of her own drama.

My friend, who is very spiritually aware and striving, realizes that to completely transform this old pattern she must master every aspect of the lesson that her soul and Higher Self are trying to teach her through this dream.

The same is true for all of us. The message may be that we need to strengthen our boundaries and claim our positive qualities. But it is also likely pointing out subtle seeds of negativity within us that are acting like magnets to draw negative energy from other people.

There is an ancient principle of energy exchange, "Like attracts like," meaning that we attract to us the same kind of energy we are carrying within us. This is why a person who is angry typically attracts angry or provocative people. Or the flip side, an angry person may attract passive people, who are easily victimized.

Lessons of Forgiveness

My client Marie had recurring nightmares of being tortured, similar to Natalie, whom we talked about earlier. In the course of analyzing her nightmares and doing trauma-release work, Marie discovered that the nightmares were bringing two major lessons to her.

The first was that she had to stand, face and conquer her own inner torturer, the negative animus. In her case this was a habit of condemning and guilt-tripping herself for not being perfect. She simply wouldn't forgive herself when she made *any* mistake. She was literally torturing herself with guilt and self-doubt.

The second lesson appeared when Marie remembered a past-life experience where she had been tortured to death at the time of the Inquisition. She realized these dreams were telling her she was still carrying that energy and her reaction to it at an unconscious level. Once she released the past-life record through trauma-release work and violet-flame transmutation,[2] she stopped having the nightmares.

Marie also began a solid program of healing the inner torturer. She first had to realize and accept that everyone makes mistakes, that no one is perfect in the human condition. That was quite difficult for Marie.

Gradually she began to understand that her sense of perfection and nonforgiveness was simply a part of the inner torturer; it didn't mean she was a bad person. She went through a profound forgiveness ritual in which she asked God to forgive her and felt the return current of divine forgiveness. Then she realized that if God could forgive her mistakes, she certainly could forgive herself. So she did. But it took a lot of reinforcement because her nonforgiveness was so ingrained.

Marie would affirm every day that her perfection was in her soul's union with her Higher Self and that she, as a daughter of the Father-Mother God, was worthy of forgiveness. She began to recite daily a very simple affirming formula: "I will do my best, call it good and ask God to handle the rest. If I make a mistake, I will ask for forgiveness, I will accept forgiveness and I will choose to forgive myself. I will strive to learn the soul lessons I need in order to claim my victory. And I claim my victory today!"

Each evening she began her prayers by asking for and accepting forgiveness for her human mistakes. Then she consciously forgave anyone who had been unkind to her. She also gave a rosary to the Blessed Mother[3] once a week, during which she consciously surrendered her desire for human perfection and prayed for the perfection of her soul.

Gradually Marie began to resolve the torturous problem of perfectionism. In due time, she came to realize that she had been playing God with herself by trying to be perfect. And there was no way to win that one!

Spiritually, she needed to surrender her pride in perfectionism as well as her tormentor-victim consciousness. In turn, she needed to draw upon the inner strength, wisdom and love of her Higher Self to treat herself more compassionately.

Was there a central lesson to this drama? Yes. It was all about accepting that she is a lovable child of God, and that it is okay to love herself. All of her life she had found it much easier to love other people than to love herself. Once she decided she was lovable, because she had been created that way, it made all the difference.

Learning to Love and Care for Ourselves

I believe that learning to love and care for ourselves is a major lesson for all of us. We all need to learn how to love ourselves as God loves us. How do we get there?

First, we accept that we are children of divine love. Then, we choose to live the teaching to "love one another." As we do so on a daily basis, we become more and more attuned with the higher vibrations of cosmic love.

On a practical level, this means we cultivate loving,

harmonious relationships with ourselves, our friends and family. And we adopt an attitude of harmlessness and good will toward all.

For some people, loving themselves can be the greatest challenge of all. How do we begin?

I suggest to my clients that they begin with their dream messages—understanding them and deciding to transform any negatives that have surfaced in them, as did Marie. Second, I explain that at an energetic level, their body is the ultimate receptor of their unresolved negatives, whether in motivations, attitudes, mind-sets, emotional reactions or physical habits.

Third, I suggest they accept their Higher Self as their partner and develop spiritual practices that will strengthen their creative, positive energy and transmute (transform) the daily negative residue. Fourth, I suggest they focus on positive thoughts and compassionate feelings and take constructive action whenever necessary. Fifth, I recommend they follow a balanced diet, get regular exercise, proper sleep and periodically go on a fast (one to three days) to cleanse the physical body of toxins.* Adepts over the ages have used such practices as transformational rituals.

Does all of this work? Yes. Research increasingly demonstrates that a positive attitude, healing imagery and focused prayer help us heal physically, mentally and emotionally. Whether we are at home, in the workplace or even in the health practitioner's office, we can practice positive affirma-

*Consult your physician prior to fasting and cleansing if you have a medical condition or are pregnant or a nursing mother.

tion, creative imagery, constructive mental attitude and heart-to-heart interaction.[4]

Research from HeartMath Institute in Boulder Creek, California, shows that relating from the heart is not only emotionally satisfying but also can be physically healing.[5]

Techniques such as spiritual visualization, guided imagery, color and music therapy, emotional-release techniques and massage therapy are proving to be effective in restoring health and vigor. Healing modalities such as acupuncture, acupressure and energy medicine are gaining increased respect and popularity. They work to adjust the flow of the subtle life energy through the meridians.

Holistic doctors are consulted more and more by people looking for natural alternatives to drug therapy. Many chiropractors now work with redirecting the body's energy flow in addition to adjusting the physical body.

All of these approaches are ultimately ways of drawing upon our higher spiritual energy to correct the subtle energy flow into our mind, emotions and physical body. The bottom line is that when we exercise right spirit, right mind, right desiring and right action, we bring healing energy into our world.

When healing energy enters our world, we experience more peaceful dreams and are much more likely to have positive dreams than nightmares. If we do have a nightmare, though, we recognize we are facing a part of ourselves that we need to challenge and transform. The transformational process itself becomes a spiritual exercise.

The Creative Power of Sound

What kind of exercises can we do to help this along? We can treat our dreams as both real and symbolic—real in the sense of the positive and negative aspects of our personality, symbolic in the sense of metaphorical lessons for our soul development.

We can use prayers, mantras and decrees to invoke light and to transmute the uncomfortable aspects of our dreams once we have some understanding of their message. An effective way to do this is to focus the mind on spiritual concepts and combine that with the use of the creative power of sound.

As did the adepts of old, we can commune with Spirit through prayer. And we can direct God's light into our lives and circumstances through the creative power of mantra. What kind of light is it? It is the subtle energy that Eastern traditions call *ch'i* or *prana*. It is a spiritual way to "lighten up!"

One of my favorite ways of doing this is through the I AM mantras. When we give these mantras, especially ones invoking the white or violet light, we can transform negative vibrations and patterns in our thoughts, feelings and physical habits. I find the white light, which includes all of the colors of the spectrum, and the violet light are particularly transformational.

When I say, "I AM ___," I am saying, "God in me is ___." For example, "I AM loving to everyone" means "God in me is loving to everyone." "I AM light" means "God in me is light."

Each one of us has a divine spark of light at the core of our being. So through I AM affirmations we can invoke that power of God's light within us to transform any negatives that are happening, including negative conditions, thoughts, feelings or dysfunctional behavior. We can also create I AM affirmations to help us develop the positive patterns.

Here is a series of affirmations put together in what is known as a decree. This decree is a way to petition God, the great I AM, to direct spiritual light into whatever problem situation we may be facing. As I recite the decree, I affirm that all negative intent and darkness in that circumstance is consumed and replaced by God's intention and light. I visualize each concept as I voice it.

> I AM light, glowing light, radiating light, intensified light!
> God consumes my darkness, transmuting it into light.
> This day I AM a focus of the Central Sun.
> Flowing through me is a crystal river,
> A living fountain of light
> That can never be qualified by human thought or feeling.
> I AM an outpost of the divine.
> Such darkness as has used me is swallowed up
> By the mighty river of light which I AM.
> I AM, I AM, I AM light! I live, I live, I live in light!
> I AM light's fullest dimension;
> I AM light's purest intention.
> I AM light! light! light!
> Flooding the world everywhere I move,
> Blessing, strengthening and conveying
> The purpose of the kingdom of heaven.[6]

This decree, this series of I AM affirmations, says it all for me because it affirms my vision of our soul's destiny on Earth and path homeward to God. As you speak the words aloud, visualize yourself enveloped in brilliant white light that shimmers with all of the colors of the rainbow.

Through the alchemy of divine light invoked by a spoken decree and combined with visualization, whatever is less than God's light at that moment is transformed into a higher vibration.

I believe this is why the great avatars and saints are frequently depicted with a halo, which has been described as the opened crown chakra or an aura of light.[7] The adept's energy field has become one with the light of Spirit, which transmutes all darkness. As a more homely example, it's a bit like turning on the light in a dark room. Where does the darkness go? Nowhere really. It is simply transformed into light.

Here is another I AM mantra I like to give every day because violet flame is the action of the Holy Spirit when it is dissolving all that is not of God's light. I find it to be truly transformational.

> I AM the violet flame in action in me now,
> I AM the violet flame, to light and love I bow.
> I AM the violet flame in mighty cosmic power,
> I AM the light of God shining every hour.
> I AM the violet flame blazing like a sun,
> I AM God's sacred power freeing everyone.[8]

Some years ago, I had a client, Irene, who was a checker in a large grocery store. She would come in for her therapy sessions feeling out of sorts because of the mayhem, as she put it, in the checkout lines. She said it was particularly awful when parents with children would come through and the children wanted something the parents didn't want them to have, or when the parent would be frazzled and short-tempered from the stress of the shopping excursion.

I taught Irene a short violet-flame mantra, "I AM a being of violet fire. I AM the purity God desires."[9] I suggested that she give it a number of times each morning as she was driving to work. I also suggested that she visualize each of the shoppers coming through her checkout line surrounded with violet light, especially when they seemed frazzled. She was really good at visualizing so I knew she would be able to do it.

Irene came in the next week laughing as she told me what had happened. She said, "I did it, and I couldn't believe it! People started calming down. Children stopped screaming. It was like a different world with people coming through my checkout line. I had a great week. God must really want me to be doing this because every time I'd forget to give the mantra, the mayhem would start coming back. It's almost like magic."

I assured her it wasn't magic, but it was the alchemy of the light of God changing the energy field around her and her checkout stand. As we use this ancient method of invoking spiritual light through the creative power of visualization and sound, we become as the master alchemist transmuting the energies of darkness into light.

Since such transmutation takes place at the energetic level, we can also use this means to change our prickly attitudes, stubborn mind-sets, emotional hot buttons and self-sabotaging behaviors. We can be delivered from burdensome conditions that oppress us in our dreams, and we can replace them with God's light and love.

We can also change our behavior from being constantly on guard in a negative way to feeling inwardly empowered, making wise and diplomatic decisions and being genuinely kind, caring and forgiving to others.

As we learn to greet the unfortunate happenings in our lives with love and to create peaceful, harmonious relationships with the people we meet along the way, we better understand the lives of the avatars, saints and sages throughout history. By example they taught their followers to embody divine love and compassion. And those teachings are just as applicable today.

When we look at the lives of Paramahansa Yogananda, Mahatma Gandhi, Padre Pio, Mother Teresa, Clara Barton and Florence Nightingale, great lights of the nineteenth and twentieth centuries, we realize that each one had to make some difficult choices. No matter what the circumstances, though, they offered their love and compassion to those they met along the way. I have no doubt that the angels and higher beings were cheering wildly as these souls returned home to God as victors of divine love on Earth.

Who will be the compassionate ones in the twenty-first century? Who will choose to walk the path of divine love, to bless the earth with the healing balm of mercy and peace?

Who will graduate from this earthly plane of existence and move on to cosmic service in the "many mansions" prepared for us in the heaven world?

May our highest hopes and dreams become eternal truth as we, too, become victors of love over every shadowy circumstance in our lives.

CHAPTER EIGHT

Dreams as Messages from Higher Realms

The dream is the small hidden door in the deepest and most intimate sanctum of the soul.

—CARL GUSTAV JUNG
The Meaning of Psychology for Modern Man

*I*n his famous essay "Of Experience," Michel de Montaigne, French moralist and essayist from the 1500s, offered a key to the interpretation of our dreams that is still applicable today. He said, "Dreams are faithful interpreters of our inclinations; but there is art required to sort and understand them."[1]

Indeed this is true. Dreams do reveal our inclinations from the superconscious, conscious, subconscious and unconscious mind. Each time we lay our heads to rest, our Higher Self and our soul, hand in hand, stage a drama that is a statement about our state of consciousness, our direction in life, our virtues and flaws, and the immediate lesson our soul needs to learn.

Thus, a dream is a very personal message from the higher realms of our being. It can startle us with truth and challenge us with inner conflicts or soul dilemmas that cry for resolution. Repetitive dreams show us we have yet to understand the fullness of a particular lesson.

A Spiritual Call to Action

The superconscious is the realm of what people call high dreams, dreams of mystical experiences. Such dreams reveal inner truths and remind us of our soul's destiny. They may also reveal encounters with masters and angels in the higher schools of learning on inner planes. Often, these dreams are a spiritual call to action.

One way a dream from the superconscious shows itself is by its beautiful background setting. It is often an outdoors scene—on a mountaintop or by a beautiful flowing river. The colors may be unusually clear, bright and resplendent. The scene is filled with sunshine or brilliant light. There may be lovely trees, flowers, birds and vistas of great splendor. Often there is a special feeling of peace, serenity, inspiration and joy accompanying this kind of dream.

I remember a repetitive high dream from my childhood. I always called it my pink dream because everything in this beautiful ethereal place that I would go to, night after night, was enveloped in a shimmering, misty-pink glow. Love and light were the essence of this comforting world. (The artist who did the cover painting for this book captured some of that essence.)

I would go to bed early because I wanted to visit my pink world. I still treasure that etheric experience, which reassured me of God's love and helped me through many challenging times.

I realized early on that I was meant to offer love to people in whatever ways I could. Like most of us trying to master our soul's lessons, I won some rounds and lost others. But I have never forgotten the bliss of the sublime love world, a divine heritage I believe is meant for each one of us.

It is taking a lifetime to discover all the ways that the love of God may flow through my heart. What have I learned? When love is not flowing through me, I need to figure out how I am blocking it. When I remove the block, the flow of divine love is always right there. I believe this is true for all of us as beloved children of God.

What else happens in a dream from the superconscious? Sometimes we find ourselves climbing a majestic mountain. Such mountains almost always suggest a higher state of consciousness. Our progress, or lack of it, may be indicated by the feelings we have in the dream, the way we are climbing or the heights we attain. We also discover important lessons in the obstacles that may lie in our path.

Some mystical dream symbols are relatively universal. For instance, when we dream of swimming through sparkling waters, we are likely feeling our higher emotions. If we are sailing a boat over peaceful waters, we are experiencing ourselves not only as the captain of our ship but also as a person who is at peace, emotionally.

Rainbows in the sky often herald promises or blessings. A ray of sunlight may symbolize inner wisdom, knowledge or enlightenment. Thus, mystical dreams are inspirational and can preview the emotional heights our soul may attain.

Our feelings at the end of such dreams usually indicate how we are doing in the earthly part of our trek upward. If we wake up happy and eager to go on with our day, we are in sync with our soul and moving along on the upward trail. When we awaken sad, depressed or gloomy, it is an inner flag that we are out of sync with our higher desires or are involved in something detrimental to our spiritual growth.

We may have so-called astral dreams, dreams of confusing or misshapen images, frightening or unholy circumstances, dreams from the shadowy depths. These also relate to our destiny and call us to action. How is this true? Whatever we dream—we are! We are each image, high or low, beautiful or outrageously ugly.

When we dream of beautiful images, we are seeing our divine potential, our inner wholeness and beauty, our true being. When we dream of ugly images, we are seeing parts of ourselves that we have distorted or ignored, dimensions of ourselves that are in need of healing and redemption.

Sometimes these dreams are the greatest benefit of all because they wake us up to the need to heal these wounded parts of ourselves. As we do so, we become aware that everything we think, feel, say or do that is not congruent with who we really are becomes a kind of bondage. How good it feels to free ourselves from the bondage of old hurts and dysfunctional reactions.

Evelyn's Parachute

I remember the superconscious dream of an older woman, Evelyn, who is very serious on her spiritual path but suffers at times from fear and depression. Before going to bed one night, she asked God to help her let go of these feelings.

In the morning she remembered this dream: "I'm jumping out of an airplane. My chute doesn't open properly, and I land in a black ocean. I start swimming. When I wake up, my heart is not beating fast at all and I'm surprised about that."

As Evelyn free-associated to the elements of the dream, we came to the following conclusions: The airplane represents the part of her that likes to fly high and get above it all. It's her masculine spirit side. Getting above it all can be either good or not so good. It's good if she's getting higher perspective, not so good if she's just flying around somewhere, ungrounded. Evelyn most identifies with the person jumping out of the plane, scared but willing to take a big risk. The black ocean represents dark, gloomy feelings, a depression that sometimes feels endless and overwhelming.

The parachute is lifesaving if she's going to take a huge jump from the heights of her spiritual moorings into the depths of the inner darkness she seeks to understand and navigate. The parachute represents the inner knowledge she needs to get through the jump. It's as if Evelyn is saying to herself, "I can't just think my way through this fear and depression. I have to jump in and resolve it. I have a parachute of inner understanding that will keep me connected to my spiritual being."

The chute not opening as expected represents Evelyn's fear that she might not have enough understanding to stay connected. However, as she shows herself in the dream (by swimming, not drowning), she does have enough understanding to land safely, just no extra. She is making herself aware that she needs to keep developing her spiritual understanding.

As we analyzed swimming versus sinking, Evelyn came to this further understanding: "It's interesting that I don't drown in the deep water. I don't even think about it. I just start swimming. It's like I'm not giving in to that black ocean of depression. Instinctively, I'm a survivor and I feel pretty good about that. I like feeling that I can take that big a risk and survive."

Evelyn is receiving an important transformational message through this dream. She is saying, "I know how to aim high, face what I fear, understand what I need to do and take appropriate action. As I trust my higher instincts and keep on moving, I can conquer the hobgoblins of fear and depression."

Evelyn's dream is showing her in a dramatic way that she can make it through the emotional obstacles she is encountering on her spiritual journey. Even though she may dip into fear and depression at times, she can swim safely through these deep waters if she claims her courage and strength—and trusts in her higher instincts as guidance from higher realms.

Dream Scenarios Key Us into Inner Dilemmas

Dream scenarios are not to be taken as "gospel truth" or as absolute prognostications but rather as a key to inner dilemmas—and waking behaviors that are related. They are often vivid and creative dramas. In the dream every figure and every object is a part of us.

I recall a dream I had when I first realized this truth. In the dream I was happily running down a grassy hill only to see looming ahead of me a big mud hole. I couldn't stop in time, so I ended up falling into the mud hole. When I awoke, I decided to analyze the dream. I took the dream apart, piece by piece, and tried to find the connecting points within myself.

First of all there was the part of me that I completely identified with—me running down the hill, my happy, carefree, speeding-along self. That part was fairly easy to understand and rather pleasant. Other parts of the dream, like the hill and the grassy slope, were also positive dimensions of me.

I realized that the hill represented a height of mastery I had attained, and the grassy slope was my life force growing lushly beneath my feet. I also knew that the feet can symbolize understanding, and my understanding was thus moving me forward. The height of the hill had given me a momentum that was also carrying me forward. The only problem was that it was carrying me forward—downhill—blissfully unaware of the mud hole ahead.

Through associating to the dream images, I realized that my tendency to unawareness was being shown to me, that when life seemed good I tended to be a Pollyanna in both the positive and negative sense. The positive was that I usually looked on the bright side of life; the negative was that I could be blissfully unaware at the same time. There I was, so busy enjoying the bright side that I didn't even realize I was traveling downhill into my dark side, the mud hole, until it was too late.

I remember the absolute shock that my happy run had ended in a mud hole without my having the least idea that mud lay ahead. The mud hole wasn't deep and it didn't ruin my day. But it certainly slowed me down and ruined my clothes, symbolizing my persona, the way I tried to show myself to other people—and to myself.

I realized that "slow down" was a major message for me at that time in my life. I had, in fact, been moving too fast in a lot of ways, which created some pitfalls when I didn't make the wisest decisions. Then I would get upset with myself, and other people would get upset with me.

The mud was a combination of dirt and water, representing bad feeling or muck. And that was when I got the full message: When I played Pollyanna to a fault and moved too fast, I was headed for a fall and a mucky emotional reaction!

This dream also related to an experience I had when I was about nine or ten. Our family was visiting Meteor Crater, the site in Arizona where a meteor had once struck the earth. We had climbed to the top and were on our way back down. My sister and I were pretending to skate through the crumbling rocky fragments, having a great time, when all of a sudden my feet started going faster than my head and I tumbled, head over heels, down the entire slope. I was bruised, scraped and scared but not seriously damaged.

The point here is that I was completely caught up in my good time with my feet moving faster than the rest of me— and great was the fall thereof! At times my mind can also race ahead like that, and I can end up falling flat in other ways. So my dream actually related to current situations and also reflected back to an early life experience. I still needed to learn the lesson to be on the lookout for potential obstacles and to slow down.

Shortly after the dream, in one of those synchronistic experiences, I was in a bookstore and came across a parchment poster that had the poem on it, "Slow Me Down, Lord." I put it up in my office and read it every day. I tried to remember to act on it. And I did.

This is an example of a ritual that I put into my life to help me remember the message of my dream. Every now and then, that dream and my experience at Meteor Crater come back to my awareness to remind me, metaphorically, of just what might happen if I allow my mind (or my feet!) to outrun the rest of me.

So we can see that dreams are, first of all, the staging of our own superconscious, subconscious and unconscious dramas, yet they also relate to conscious patterns of behavior that we need to resolve. Someone else who had the mud hole dream might have a completely different interpretation.

Each of us has our own way of symbolizing our life experiences—the heights and depths, the joys and sorrows. Each of us has our own way of staging a drama that is a metaphor for some dilemma of our soul and spirit.

The Elements in Our Dreams Are Who We Are

As we have seen, one of the most important principles of dream interpretation is that each person and object in the dream symbolizes a dimension of who we are. The person we identify with in the dream is the part of us that we most easily accept—even though we are actually everybody and everything else, too.

When we understand our inner drama and the different elements of our being that are portrayed, we have a major key to interpreting the dream. And many times our dreams show us a need for self-transformation.

One of my clients, Mary, reported the following dream glyph that makes the point. She dreamed that her spiritual guru, a woman, was submerged in a trench of icy water but came up laughing.

Mary associated to the elements of her dream: "My spiritual teacher has great mastery, a wonderful sense of humor and great spiritual attainment. She represents to me the highest development a woman can attain.

"A trench is something I'd build for protection, like in a war to keep from getting shot. The trench isn't really any protection at all because a person could drown or freeze to death in those icy waters. Water for me always represents emotions. So icy water would be half-frozen emotions. She came up laughing. I'd likely be shaking and swearing."

I asked Mary, "What might be the dream message? What are you saying to yourself through this dream?"

She pondered silently for a while, began to smile and replied, "I know what it is. My guru is telling me to identify with her to get through threatening situations instead of freezing in fear, getting angry or ending up immobilized. In my dream she represents my higher feminine qualities, my joy and laughter, which have been submerged these days. If I claim them, I can say, 'Scary situations have no power over me, and they cannot drown my joy.' It's a big lesson."

I asked, "How might you bring out your joy and laughter in a threatening situation?"

Mary replied, "I do have a good sense of humor, but I tend to lose it when I get really upset. I don't like feeling upset so I freeze my emotions. Instead of doing that, I could let my sense of humor and inner joy work for me. It's like laughing at the human condition at the same time as I stay in touch with my feelings.

"When I'm laughing, the fear and anger can't control me. I'm going to practice until my sense of humor is my natural response when something goes wrong. I'll be like the laughing Buddha, feminine style. That'll be some transformation!"

Judith's Transformational Dream Experience

Here is another transformational dream from a young woman, Judith—one that she considers a call from her soul and Higher Self to "wake up and get moving."

Judith described a multi-level dream that represents her present life, her childhood and her wishes for the future: "I am looking at a house with three levels. The main floor looks like a nice, normal house. The second floor is leaking and there's a fine mist over everything. It apparently wasn't finished because you can see boards and exposed wiring. The third floor is where I'd like to live. It's bigger than the other floors, unfinished, but at least it isn't leaking. I think to myself, 'O dear, if this is the state of my consciousness, leaks and unfinished rooms, I have to fix it.'

"It's crowded on the main floor and I'm looking for a room where I can have my own space. The second floor reminds me of our attic in my childhood home—full of boxes of Christmas tree stuff, old dolls and stuffed toys. The stairs going up to the third floor are more like a ladder than steps. I'm thinking, 'If I move to the third floor, it's going to be difficult to get my furniture up there.'"

I asked Judith for her associations to the three floors of the house. She closed her eyes and responded as if she were walking through the dream house: "This first floor is about my everyday life, crowded with everything I'm trying to do. It's nice and practical, but there's not much space for my creativity.

"The second floor is about my childhood wish to have the attic fixed up for me. It means childhood dreams, Christmas, toys, space for myself. It's definitely what my inner child likes. The mist here is getting everything all wet, but it feels kind of good. I think it's me crying for the good parts of my childhood and also for the dreams that weren't fulfilled—mostly having to do with my own space, space to be who I am.

"That's what the third floor is all about, who I am as an adult seeking oneness with my higher consciousness. Living up high, looking out at the trees and birds, almost touching the clouds and the sky connects me with my spiritual nature. So the third floor is my sacred space. It's what will make my soul happy while I continue to tend my inner child and do the practical things that are necessary in my daily life."

Judith's dream message was very clear to her: "I am preparing to live my dreams." She is in a three-stage process: healing the hurts and fulfilling the dreams of her childhood; expanding and realizing her vision of her soul's desires; and integrating all of this with the necessary responsibilities of her adult life.

Thus, as Judith processes and transforms the sadness from childhood, she fixes the leaks on the second floor. As she seeks to understand the connections between her childhood upbringing and her adult behavior, she repairs the wiring. As she envisions and possibly creates shelves for her childhood treasures—the dolls, special toys and Christmas decorations—she lovingly acknowledges and nurtures her inner child.

Judith's third-floor restoration is a redemptive process for her soul. She envisions bringing beauty and spaciousness into her life: "I can arrange the third floor according to feng shui techniques and bring in plants, flowers and one of those indoor fountains. I'll have beautiful paintings of nature, angels and mystical settings on my walls. I'll have my piano, my lovely old furniture and my own library in this higher space. It's like bringing out the beauty and culture that are the essence of my higher consciousness."

The final stage of this dream work is for Judith to express her soul's hopes and dreams as she fulfills her daily responsibilities. She decided, "I need to integrate the three floors of my being. The main floor is my daily practical doings, so necessary to my marriage and career. The second floor is my inner child work. And the third floor is my soul's integration with my Higher Self. I need easy access to all three floors of my being—and that is going to be priority for me."

Judith truly understood her "wake-up call" and is determined to act upon it. As she does so, step-by-step, she will be healing her childhood hurts and meeting the spiritual needs of her soul.

Gifts and Protection for a Woman Walking the Mystical Path

Another woman, Amber, had a series of dreams from higher realms that offered gifts and protection. She is an older woman who from childhood has cultivated spiritual wisdom in the face of physical and emotional difficulties. Her greatest joy comes from communing with God and sharing her spiritual insights with others.

In a dream about her spiritual calling, she saw Aristotle being given a magnificent ring in a velvet box. The ring had a huge ruby in the center. She said, "It wasn't for me, but I wanted to try it on. On my hand, it became a gold band with little rubies in it. I am very happy that Aristotle is getting the ring."

In free-associating to the dream, Amber said she has always looked for her other half, in this case, her Higher Self. She has always read a great deal and loves Socrates' teachings, which were written down by Plato and passed on by Aristotle.

In this dream, Aristotle represents her Higher Self. She sees the rubies as symbolizing the precipitation of God's fiery love. Their setting in a gold ring represents the wedding of her fiery love for God with a state of golden illumination.

The rubies also symbolize a "ruby ray" path, the adepts' path of sacrifice, surrender, selflessness and service.[2] She sees it as a mystical calling to sacrifice her lesser self to God, to surrender all that might prevent her soul's reunion with God, to be selfless in her motivations and desires, and to serve people lovingly as she meets them along life's way.

The dream indicates that her Higher Self has earned the gift. She, as the soul who is striving, is allowed to try it on and is happy her Higher Self is receiving it. The implication is that if she continues to serve others with love, to walk the ruby ray path, then someday her soul too may earn the jewel of divine love.

Amber has also had several dreams about diamonds, which represent to her the mystical consciousness of God. In one dream she is given a huge diamond that is made up of a lot of tiny sparkling diamond fragments. Someone takes the diamond fragments away, exposing an ancient ring with the Star of David and the Christian cross on it.

She said of this dream, "I was raised a traditional Jew but later followed the Christian teachings. All my life I have sought the inner mystical teachings wherever I could find them. The mystical teachings are the beautiful jewels in each of the world's religions."

Amber believes the diamond fragments represent the diamond-shining mind of God, multiplied and scattered worldwide as tiny fragments of light and truth. She sees how her earlier spiritual walk with Judaism and Christianity helped prepare her for inner mystical understanding. The Star of David and the Christian cross in the dream represent her spiritual foundations.

This same theme appears in another dream glyph where Amber sees a thick chain of diamonds that has a twenty-four-carat diamond pendant on it. She feels blessed to be seeing the diamonds of God's consciousness and says, "It's like I'm experiencing the etheric world touching down into the physical."

In keeping with this, Amber awakened one morning with an image of two golden books. She was seeing them while her eyes were still closed. She told me she loves old books, books with spiritual teachings in them. She said such golden books as she saw would be filled with illumination and precious mystical teachings.

A dream of a different kind, but also in keeping with Amber's spiritual path, was about divine protection in the face of evil. She dreamed that she was in a house with other spiritual people. They were being bombarded by evil beings. Then she saw a magnificent, white lion outside. He was standing very still and she realized he was their divine protector.

As she processed the dream, Amber recognized that the spiritual people in it were different dimensions of her soul pursuing God's truth. The evil beings represented archetypal figures from her personal unconscious as well as the collective unconscious. They opposed the light and would prevent her from knowing divine truth.

The white lion was the protector of her light. His stance of stillness represented courage, alertness and the stilling of the mind. The lion also symbolized for her a modern-day adept and master, Mark Prophet, whom she reveres for his courage and strength of heart.[3]

The fact that she was relatively unperturbed by the bombardment from these evil beings says that she did not allow them to have power over her. Instead, she focused her attention on the divine protector.

Preparing for High Dreams and Etheric Experiences

While our body sleeps, we may be instructed in spiritual truths by our Higher Self or by the angels and ascended masters. If we explore our thoughts and feelings upon awakening, we may remember our etheric experiences and spiritual insights.

Even if we don't remember them directly, we may very well wake up with an inspiring idea or a creative solution to a nagging problem. A teaching may flash into our mind that sets a positive direction for our day. Or during the day we may be inspired to take certain actions.

One key to this kind of remembrance is to practice Mother Mary's rapt attention on God. In this mode we keep the inner ear of our soul always attuned to the inspiration of the angels and the guidance of our Higher Self.

Another key is to ask God to help us remember our inner experiences and understand how to apply the guidance we receive. When we practice spiritual values and include God in our thoughts, we accelerate in higher consciousness and are more apt to remember our high dreams and etheric experiences.

CHAPTER NINE

Etheric Studies
in the Heaven World

Our birth is but a sleep and a forgetting:
The soul that rises with us, our life's star,
Hath had elsewhere its setting,
And cometh from afar.

—WILLIAM WORDSWORTH
Ode. Intimations of Immortality
from Recollections of Early Childhood

What is it like to be in the world of etheric studies? Initially it may seem very much like a dream, a really high dream, one in which we feel exalted, joyous and clear. Yet there is also a strong sense of reality and practicality. We have a sense that this is much more than a dream. We have entered a sacred space, a space of higher consciousness beyond the world as we know it.

Some have called these places spiritual retreats or universities of the Spirit.* Here inner mysteries of life are unfolded. We may meet masters, angels and other spiritual seekers. Our teachers may communicate telepathically as well as verbally. Sometimes a lesson is conveyed as an experience we go through. The knowledge gained is at once esoteric and practical, transformational and applicable to our lives.

Attuning Ourselves to the Etheric World

As we have discussed, entering into such an experience is a matter of vibration, attunement and spiritual focus. When we think about the mysteries of God and the lives of the mystics and adepts who have perceived them, we realize that these serious seekers dedicated themselves to a higher purpose. They

*Spiritual retreats are focuses of ascended beings and archangels in the heaven world. The universities of the Spirit are classes in higher truths, lessons for the soul and holy rituals taught by angels and ascended masters in the spiritual retreats.

attuned themselves to the voice of God. They focused their lives on holy matters. Thus, they prepared themselves for etheric experiences and entrance into the heaven world.

The process of inner attunement continues day and night. When we earnestly ask our Higher Self and the ascended masters to help us understand the higher mysteries of life, we cultivate a state of inner contemplation that sets the tone for etheric studies. A daily practice of meditation, prayer and spiritual reading helps us focus our attention upon the divine. Thus we prepare our consciousness to receive holy experiences.

At night we release the burdens of the day. Before going to sleep, commune with God through prayer, meditation or mantras, and visualize yourself surrounded by shimmering white light. Pray in simple words for divine guidance in your daily life and the nightly journey of your soul.

Ask the angels to escort you to the etheric retreat that God has chosen for you. Offer a prayer or give a decree to Archangel Michael and his bands,* asking them to guide you safely there. And remind yourself that you will remember your dreams or etheric experiences when you awaken in the morning. As you begin to drift off to sleep, visualize and affirm your oneness with the light. Send your heart's love to the angels, your Higher Self and your God.

During the night you may commune with the ascended masters (our elder brothers and sisters of light in the heaven world) about your life, planning and agreeing to every major event you will experience on Earth. Inwardly, at the level of

---

*See page 79.

your soul, you already know the spiritual lessons you need to learn. With the guidance of your Higher Self and the ascended masters, you may select those circumstances that are best for learning your lessons.

Upon awakening, notice and write down the first thoughts or images that come to mind. Sometimes they will be a clear retreat memory, mystical or inspirational in nature. At other times you may not remember a particular retreat experience but simply feel good or "clear" when you awaken.

When you do remember any kind of dream or impression, even if it seems mundane or astral, you will do well to write it down. Within it may be a clue to higher teachings you have received but forgotten in your return through the veils of energy between the etheric and physical planes.

If you try but do not seem to succeed, keep on asking your Higher Self and the angels to guide you to the higher realms at night. Ask for your consciousness to be attuned to the higher vibrations of the etheric realm and cleared of all density so that you may remember your journey and the instruction you receive.

You may be having retreat experiences but not recalling them, just as everyone dreams but many do not remember their dreams. Ultimately, as you continue your practice over time, you will begin to remember certain aspects of your retreat experiences, the inner mystical teachings you receive and how they apply to your daily life.

Sometimes, even when you do not remember a dream or an etheric experience, you may awaken with a clearer perspective on some detail of your life. I believe we actually chart our course through life not only by our actions in the waking state but also by the divine guidance we receive at night—whether or not we remember those experiences when we awaken.

Historically, heavenly visitations during sleep have been described as numinous dreams, dreams that are filled with light and power and the presence of the divine. The dream experience itself tells us that we stand in a holy place.

Perhaps you have had such a dream in which you traveled with an angel or entered an inner space of mystical beauty and peace. Even if you did not remember the fullness of the dream when you awoke, you likely felt a sense of deep reverence and awe. The message or lesson may have been clear in your mind when you awoke, or it may have unfolded throughout the following days and weeks.

As you continue your spiritual practices, you will remember your dreams and etheric experiences more often. You may reside in these higher planes of consciousness until you are ready to awaken in the morning.

At times you may remember only a glyph of the retreat experience, but if you treat it as a high dream and go through your associations to the elements of the dream you may recover more details and the message for your soul.

Shambhala and a Soul-Retrieval Dream

A client of mine, Sheila, experienced what she called a soul-retrieval dream. She described it to me: "I'm part of a group of people in the desert, people I teach with today. I have broken off from the others and am living in a cave. A man I love comes after me.

"I come out of the cave and I'm standing in a wooded area looking at the sky. I see bright light, stars of great beauty. As I stand there, I magnetize sparks of my soul back to my heart. I realize these are parts of my soul that have been lost since ancient times. I am retrieving the lost parts of my soul."

I asked Sheila to tell me her reflections on the dream and soul-retrieval experience. From the depths of her heart and soul she shared this profound past-life experience: "I remember leaving an ancient mystery school, Shambhala, as a result of following theories that were twisted half-truths instead of pursuing the eternal truths I had been taught. I believe I actually left parts of my soul with the false teachers I followed.

"Desert was all that was left when Shambhala moved from the physical into the etheric plane. So I think of a cave as a primitive place of shelter. I think we got that primitive when we deserted the ancient truths we had been taught. The man who comes after me in the dream reminds me of a man in this life who claimed he loved me but would never commit. Both the man in the dream and the man in my life played with my mind. And I bought into it.

"This beautiful wooded area was like the giant redwoods on the Pacific Coast. They are huge old trees that stretch toward the heavens and seem to touch the eternal. It's symbolic of what my soul yearns to do. The bright light I see in the sky is brilliant white light, which I think of as representing the world of Spirit. The stars of great beauty are like the star that guided the three wise men to the place of Jesus' birth, the star of God's presence.

"I wish with all my heart that my soul might be made whole, that I might come home to the heaven world. In the dream the sparks flying into my heart are like the sparks of the sefirot in the Kabbalah.[1] They must be the sparks of my soul that I lost when I left Shambhala."

I was deeply touched by Sheila's experience and asked if she wished to share anything more. She seemed both exhilarated and saddened when she said, "Wishes aren't enough but they indicate my earnest desire to pursue my spiritual destiny. I know I must turn my back on false teachers or people who act like them, people who play with my mind.

"I want to raise my consciousness to the starry heights of divine wisdom. I want to touch the hem of God's garment by focusing on eternal light and truth and invoking the presence of the angels to guide me home. I believe the masters and my Higher Self will help me magnetize and reclaim my ancient soul parts. I do so much want to be restored to the fullness of my soul identity and to return to oneness with the angels and my ascended brothers and sisters."

This profound dream, the combination of a past life and an etheric experience, represented a turning point for this seeker of mystical truth. As a consequence to understanding the dream, Sheila freed herself from a long-term uncommitted relationship that mirrored her ancient departure from truth.

She realizes that standing for truth has been her sacred

journey in many lives. She is determined to win her soul's victory in this life and return home to the octaves of light. She is truly a warrior of the Spirit who is striving to bring light and truth to everyone she meets along life's way.

Sometimes such revelatory dreams seem to occur as an unexpected gift, like a happy accident. In these cases, the masters appear to be offering us a hand up to the high road. For such an unexpected blessing, we can be grateful beyond measure.

More often the gift of higher awareness is given to those who have prepared their consciousness to receive it. People blessed with retreat experiences have typically prepared themselves through devotions, earnestly seeking to walk a higher way and asking their God to teach them how they might be of more help to others.

A Symbolic Lesson from a Retreat Experience

A young man, Thomas, brought a dream of an etheric retreat experience that was totally symbolic yet very real in its application to his life. As he described it, "While I was attending a spiritual conference in San Diego, I dreamed of being in an etheric retreat. I believe it was the retreat of Serapis Bey, the master of the ascension temple.[2] I saw a sphinx. A big sword was covering me from head to toe in my etheric body. I saw a big white owl and a few people walking by. Then I awoke, clear."

As Thomas associated to the dream elements, we came up with the following: The sphinx is an ancient symbol of power and authority. The sword represents taking authority or power.

It is also a ceremonial tool of spiritual adepts to cut people free from evil spirits.

The esoteric meaning of the word *sword* is "sacred word," meaning the highest authority of the word of God. The sword covering him from head to toe in his etheric body symbolizes his being repolarized to his original spiritual nature. The white owl represents pure wisdom, and the people walking around are other aspects of his spiritual nature.

I asked Thomas what the dream message was for him. He replied, "I am being pointed to my divine plan. My authority and pure wisdom come from the level of the divine. Through the sword, the sacred word, I am purified and my ancient power restored."

This young man, truly an adept in the making, knows that his deepest desire is to repolarize himself to the light of the Eternal. In his spiritual practice he uses a ceremonial sword to clear his aura of negative energies while at the same time invoking the light of God through prayers, fiats and decrees. As he continues to do his part to clear his consciousness, he is readying himself to be a pure vessel to receive the authority and wisdom of God and to fulfill his divine plan, his soul's destiny.

Mirrors of the Buddha

Another of my clients, Jennifer, who honors the teachings of the Buddha, reported a different kind of etheric experience: "I dream I am in the foyer of a temple, where there is a full-length mirror for people to see how they relate to the Buddha. I am asked to come up with two more mirrors, one as the reflector of fear, the other as a reflector of light. I say, 'No, it should be a reflector of truth. This isn't my job.' Then the mirror of the Buddha reflects my Buddha nature to show me how far I have come, but I don't remember the details. Then, I wake up."

As Jennifer doesn't remember the details of what she saw in the mirror that reflected her Buddha nature, she has not yet internalized the fullness of the Buddha's lesson. In her associations to the dream images, she sees that her objection to coming up with the mirror of fear represents a fear that her energy will disrupt the harmony of the temple.

She also realizes that she fears being noticed and that her self-consciousness, that feeling of being observed by everyone, is actually a subtle form of pride. Similarly, with the mirror of light she is concerned that the light would reveal dark momentums within her that would disturb the temple.

Even as she says, "No, this isn't my job," Jennifer realizes she is dodging the truth. Thus, her next words are that the mirror she creates should be a reflector of truth. The truth is that she needs to overcome her fears and the subtle pride that lurks behind them.

Jennifer's dream is telling her to overcome fear and pride and claim her true Buddhic nature by being completely honest with herself. She was deeply touched by this dream and determined to take action. Her resolution: "I will give the mantra to Kuan Yin of fearlessness to help overcome my fears, and I will pray to Kuan Yin of moon and water to help me banish pride."[3]

The Childlike Consciousness

Another of my clients, Laurel, was doing her morning altar work when she recalled an etheric dream of being with Babaji, a revered avatar of India.[4] As she described it, "I am with others in a beautiful outdoor setting that has a small body of water. Babaji is instructing his students and I am happy to be in his presence.

"As I observe him, he enters into profound meditation, as if in *samadhi*.[5] and then slips into the water. He reminds me of the boy who is the Buddha in the movie *The Little Buddha*. After remembering this dream, I dedicated my Lent to Babaji. Since my experience with Babaji, all I have to do is say his name and I feel him right here with me.

"Once before I remember having a dream about a master, only that time it was Gautama Buddha. He was telling me, 'We will escape the horrors of the end of the age by going into the mountain.' When I dream of a master I feel I am communing with him."

When Laurel awoke from her dream with Babaji she felt very happy; she had happy tears in gratitude to God for the dream. She sees Babaji as a great master, a personification of the Father aspect of God. Being able to say his name, Babaji, and have him immediately there verifies for her the close relationship she has with him on inner levels.

Laurel interpreted the beautiful area with a small body of water as an inspirational setting for such a high spiritual experience. She felt that the peacefulness of it represented her own sense of inner peace. Babaji meditating and slipping into the body of water was his entering into the bliss of communion with the divine Mother. He was going into samadhi, entering a blissful superconscious state of oneness with Spirit.

Babaji's appearance reminding her of the boy in *The Little Buddha* movie was a message that the childlike consciousness is the consciousness of the Buddha. She commented, "As Jesus says, 'A little child shall lead them.' I am like a child inside. It is the innocence of my child-consciousness that opens my spiritual senses."

The words of Gautama Buddha, "Escape the horrors of the end of the age by going into the mountain" meant to Laurel that people move beyond fear of calamity, old age and death by entering into union with God, the mountain of God's consciousness. Laurel said that when she dreams of a master and communes with him, she experiences a transfer of his light, energy and consciousness and this strengthens her connection with her own Higher Self.

What was Laurel's dream message? As she spoke it, "God is a mystery, the author of all science and religion. God is also very personal and appears through masters and teachers I can identify with. I touch the garment of God's consciousness through my high dreams and etheric experiences. I'm grateful and moved by the ever-loving presence of God. I must seek a closer communion every day through meditation, prayers, decrees and music."

A Dream Glyph of the Initiations of a Guru

Another client, Georgia, had a glyph of an etheric dream concerning her spiritual guru, who is going through intense spiritual and physical initiations that are likened to the Dark Night of the Spirit.[6]

In this glyph, the guru appears with her face disfigured, as if she doesn't want to be seen. Other people don't notice her. As my client communes with the guru, they exchange love and understanding that is beyond words.

In her meditations upon the meaning of this dream, Georgia experiences her guru as a strong warrior soul. The guru's disfigured face is but a surface appearance. It is Georgia's wounded persona being reflected in the mirror of the guru. The guru not wanting to be seen symbolizes true spirituality being a hidden mystery. Their love and understanding being beyond words indicates the depths of Georgia's love for God.

Through this dream, Georgia is telling herself to look beyond appearances to the hidden mysteries and to remember that surface wounds are not the essence of herself or her guru. Inwardly, she knows that the love and understanding she shares with her guru are the fruits of a deep, inner spirituality. This dream has strengthened her determination to commune with God daily and to continue to seek the deeper meaning of the hidden mysteries.

Etheric Retreats Offer Spiritual Advancement

I have had clients tell me that in their dreams I am teaching them in a class or retreat setting or that I appear in their dreams as a counselor. These images may represent our encounter on inner planes where we offer our gifts to one another, but they also represent the dreamer's own inner teacher and inner counselor.

Thus, while we visit the inner planes at night, we study, learn and do the spiritual work for which we have been trained. This is a part of the process of spiritual initiation and the advancement of our soul at inner levels.

As we become more adept in remembering our retreat experiences, we also become more comfortable with the whole process of shifting from one plane of existence to another. Eastern traditions teach that dying is moving on in consciousness, moving to another plane of existence, just as normal and effortless as going to sleep. We are also seeing this concept more and more in popular culture.

Those who live with this understanding find death simply a transition into another plane of existence. One of my dearest friends from childhood who passed on a number of years ago went this way. At the end, she looked up with a radiant expression, called out to Jesus, "I'm coming, Lord," and left her body.

Near-Death Glimpses of the Heaven World

People like Dannion Brinkley, Betty Eadie and George Ritchie have written of their near-death experiences and have gone on to devote their lives to serving others.[7]

They write about traveling through a tunnel of light and meeting with spiritual beings in the heaven world. These happenings include a life review and a decision from Higher Authority that life on Earth for them is not yet finished. I think of these near-death experiences as a special kind of retreat experience where the major lesson seems to be "You have more work to do on Earth."

I remember the story of a friend of mine, a spiritual healer, who had a near-death experience during heart surgery. She suddenly found herself transported into the presence of Mother Mary. Mary looked startled and queried, "What are *you* doing here?" At that moment my friend popped back into her body and came back to life.

This short but profound visit to the etheric realm left a lasting impression on her. She said, "I guess it wasn't my time to go. I still have work to do here." She is at peace with her understanding of God's timing.

Coming into the presence of the divine in a near-death experience is not restricted to adults. Melvin Morse, in his book *Closer to the Light,* tells of the touching experience of Tom, "a scientist of international reputation in his forties who nearly drowned at the age of five."

Tom was "pulled from a swimming pool and resuscitated by a relative. When the family finally got him to the hospital, doctors in the emergency room said he was dead. Shortly thereafter, he spontaneously revived."

Tom tells of his experience, "When I was underwater, the next thing I remembered was passing down a long tunnel. The Light went from being very harsh to so bright that I could feel it. Then I saw God on a throne. People—maybe angels—were below looking up at the throne. I sat on the lap of God, and he told me that I had to go back. 'It's not your time,' he said. I wanted to stay but I came back."

As Morse tells us, "Tom credits this experience with

'sorting out' his life. From that point on, he was driven to acquire knowledge. He decided to study science and engineering, subjects that could help him discover 'the natural order of things.' His reputation shows that he has been successful in that endeavor."[8]

Perhaps Tom's account touched me because when I prayed as a child I also envisioned God as sitting on a throne. I was below looking up at the throne. I was always in awe of that experience. God perhaps shows himself to little children in this way because it is easy for them to understand.

When I began to study esoteric teachings as an adult, I learned that the inner meaning of *throne* is three-in-one, referring to the Trinity. This idea goes with another esoteric teaching of a mystical inner room called the secret chamber of the heart. It exists in the etheric beyond time and space but is connected with our physical heart.

On an altar in that beautiful secret chamber burns the eternal flame of life that sustains our being. That flame is threefold, having plumes of blue, yellow and pink, which symbolize our own divine power, wisdom and love.[9]

Lessons for Spiritual Growth

Those who remember their etheric retreat experiences tell us that our studies begin with lessons for overall spiritual growth. We also have practical lessons on how to resolve specific problems we are facing in our lives. Often the two are interwoven as we realize that a problem in our waking life has been an inner push to learn a spiritual lesson.

While still visiting the inner planes, we may also have opportunity to practice the lessons we've just learned. Sometimes we may give help to people, especially those for whom we have been praying. We may work with healing or counseling for our family, friends or even strangers.

During a retreat experience, several possibilities or alternatives to a puzzling situation may be reviewed. Eventually the best one is chosen and by morning we awaken with a needed answer, or at least a workable theory to try. We may awaken with an aspect of a problem solved or a forgotten fact recalled. Most of the time we arise totally unaware of the learning that has taken place at deeper levels, yet we may have just worked out a very satisfying solution to a problem we couldn't handle the day before.

At times we may recall attending classes at one of the universities of the Spirit. We may even remember some of the ascended masters or fellow classmates who were there. Or we may remember the essence of the spiritual lesson even if we don't consciously remember the retreat experience.

However, it is also possible that we remember neither the etheric experience nor the specific instruction. We may not even remember dreaming, much less a solution to a problem. But when we face the puzzling situation again, we get a new idea or a flash of inspiration. We suddenly know exactly what to do. Here is an example of that scenario.

My client, Jeff, came in excited to share something with me. He said, "I had a profound experience this week that you won't believe. As you know, I've been trying every way I can to get through this trap of a job that I'm in. The system just does-n't allow change.

"The other day I was being confronted by my supervisor about some work that isn't finished because I have more work assigned than I can get done in a timely manner. And I don't have any help with it. I really couldn't think of anything at all to say in my defense because we've been over this before.

"Suddenly as I was listening to him go on and on, I was prompted to pray to God for help right then and there. Silently I did just that, and as I did so, this dream glyph from the night before came back to me. I hadn't remembered it until this job confrontation was going on.

"In this glyph I am in a castle high up on a mountain and there is no way out. I try every way I know, but there's still no way out. I decide the only thing to do is pray. I pray and all of a sudden I'm out of there and free.

"This goes through my mind as a flash as I'm praying for guidance and my supervisor is still at it. All of a sudden he stops, smiles compassionately and says, 'I realize this really isn't your fault. You have too many assignments and no one to help you. Let's see what we can work out.'

"I'm almost dumbfounded, going through this experience of being three places at once: with my supervisor, who is for no apparent reason doing a lightning mind-shift; outside the dream castle, breathing free; and still silently praying. What a profound experience! We worked it out with no problem.

"I went outside afterward and thanked God from the depths of my heart and soul. That's a lesson I'm never going to forget. The call really does compel the answer."

Seldom do we stop to realize where our intuitive response comes from or to connect our response with our dream life. Jeff hadn't consciously remembered the dream until he intuitively started to pray, but his soul remembered. I find over and over again that when we travel to the inner retreats of the masters, we find all knowledge available to us.

Many so-called geniuses are people who bring back information from their dream states, often from visits to the classrooms of the Spirit. It is said that at least 50 percent of all creative ideas, art, music and inventions come from dreams, especially high dreams (our visits with the masters or our Higher Self) and journeys to the etheric realm.

Albert Einstein, one of the greatest physicists of all time, often said that his solutions came as signs and images. For example, his insight into the relativity of time came from a daydream in which he saw a person riding on a beam of light.[10]

The great inventor Thomas Edison also knew and respected the knowledge available through dreams. He kept a cot in his office so he could take catnaps. While he slept he would get new ideas or solutions to puzzling scientific dilemmas.

Dwelling in the Consciousness of God

Avatars and adepts have always cultivated higher awareness through regular spiritual practices. Do you remember Luke's report of Jesus' experience on the Mount of Transfiguration?

The Bible records, "He took Peter and John and James

and went up into a mountain to pray. And as he prayed, the fashion of his countenance was altered, and his raiment was white and glistering. And, behold, there talked with him two men, which were Moses and Elias, who appeared in glory, and spake of his decease which he should accomplish at Jerusalem.

"But Peter and they that were with him were heavy with sleep; and when they were awake, they saw his glory, and the two men that stood with him."[11]

We see Jesus conversing with Moses and Elijah (Elias), who came to prepare him for the events to come in Jerusalem. Why was Jesus able to do this when his companions could not even stay awake?

Jesus as the great avatar and adept had prepared himself through his spiritual path. Thus, he was in a higher vibration. Jesus had the attunement and spiritual focus that allowed him to experience the tremendous light and numinous presence of Moses and Elijah in an alert, awake state.

Peter, John and James went to sleep in the presence of that light. They almost missed the whole show. They caught but a brief glimpse of Jesus' two companions before they departed. Jesus was dwelling in the consciousness of God while his companions caught only a glimpse of that consciousness.

The great adept Kuthumi (Koot Hoomi), whose work is known through Theosophy and other esoteric teachings, beautifully describes dwelling in the consciousness of God:

> To dwell in the consciousness of the living God is to hold oneself in a state of such constant beauty as defies description in ordinary words, in ordinary tongues.

Only the tongues of angels could even begin to describe what it is really like to have the vast power-flow of Eternity resident within the soul, to have access to the great libraries of heaven with all of the considerations and works of the sons of God recorded there, to be able to glean therefrom the fruit of a continually self-renewing knowledge and to know that his laws are divine coordinates.

These coordinates are fixed as stars in the firmament—blazing points of light that will gladden the eyes of each little child who shall come to this knowledge of himself. . . .

The alternate pleasures and displeasures that come to mankind—holding him now in the hot water of fear and then in the cool water of hope—are a source of continual pressure-pain.

But he whose delight is in the law of God and in the power of God's mind is content to convey to all generations the laws of the many mansions of the Father that gleam in the heavens and that continue to bespeak promise to the souls of men. . . .

In a very real sense the higher laws and the higher virtues are polestars to guide the mariners in this world toward their eternal realities.[12]

CHAPTER TEN

Lucid Dreaming and Tibetan Yoga

Was it a vision, or a waking dream?
Fled is that music:—Do I wake or
sleep?

—JOHN KEATS
Ode to a Nightingale

*U*nlike ordinary dreams, which seem real to the sleeper dreaming them, lucid dreams occur when the sleeper suddenly becomes aware within the dream that the experience *is* a dream. Lucid dreamers often speak of the vivid quality of their dreams, which may elicit even stronger emotional reactions than nonlucid dream experiences.

In lucid dreaming, we observe our dreams even as we participate in them. Practiced lucid dreamers can even become directors of the drama, changing the behavior of the characters and the direction or outcome of the dream. It's as if the dreamer were making an interactive movie, creating and directing a fantasy and watching it unfold at the same time.

If you are processing emotions from daytime events, you have an opportunity in a lucid dream to change an outcome for the better. If you are in the middle of a nightmare, you can query the shadowy phantom to discover its purpose. If you are having a retreat experience in a classroom with an ascended master, you can ask questions, remember the answers and apply the lessons in your waking life.

Interestingly, lucid dreaming is a skill we can learn. In fact, according to one report in 1989, 58 percent of all men and women spontaneously experience a lucid dream at least once in their lives.[1]

Training Yourself for Lucid Dreaming

To train yourself for lucid dreaming, start by keeping a dream journal. As you record your dreams, associations and dream messages over time, you will begin to recognize themes that repeat themselves. You will also become increasingly familiar with your own dream symbolism.

At times you will recognize a similarity in a dream's story to one you have had in the past. When you compare the two, you can see what progress you may be making in resolving a particular soul drama. Keeping a dream journal also helps to improve your dream recall.

Next, bring lucid dreaming into your waking life. Ask yourself several times a day, "Am I dreaming?" or "Is this a dream?" As you do this, look around and note the details of where you are and what is going on. You are training yourself to do the same in your dreams.

At the same time you are doing this, try to imagine that you are actually in a dream, that everything you perceive, including your own body, is an element of your dream. In a way this is not so unusual. Masters and adepts liken existence on Earth to a dream and God's kingdom to reality. They teach that God's kingdom is similar to what we experience in our high dreams and our visits to the etheric retreats.

When you ask yourself, "Am I dreaming?" focus not only on what is happening at the moment but also on past events that come to mind. In every situation that seems somewhat dreamlike or whenever you experience powerful emotions, say to yourself, "This is all a dream." If you have recurring dreams or dream images, ask yourself if you are dreaming whenever you encounter that image in your daily life.

By imagining you are having one of your dream experiences when you are awake, you are thinning the barrier between your waking and dreaming state. You are training yourself in waking life to respond to your dream life. Gradually your consciousness begins to get it. It becomes easier to ask yourself in a dream, "Am I dreaming?" When the answer is, "Yes," you have entered the lucid dream state.

One of my friends had an amusing experience with this. She was determined to master lucid dreaming and was practicing diligently. One night she suddenly was there. She was going through some dramatic event in her dream and suddenly realized she was observing herself at the same time. She got so excited, she shouted, *"Yes!"* and instantly returned to her body.

So much for her lucid dream that time. My friend saw the humor in it and also learned a lesson. Lucid dreaming can instantly be transformed into a waking state when it is interrupted by the enthusiastic conscious mind.

Before drifting off to sleep, tell yourself that you are going to be conscious in your dream. Use the same prompt if you awaken in the morning knowing you have been dreaming and feel as though you are falling back to sleep. Try to hold a strong visualization as you drift off to sleep. My favorite way of doing this is to close my eyes, envision brilliant shimmering light around me and softly whisper the "I AM Light" decree that I described on page 127.

When I go to sleep in the middle of this meditation, I often have a high dream or lucid dream experience. I believe this is because I am transforming my consciousness into a higher vibration, into one similar to the etheric world. By so doing I prepare myself to enter that higher vibratory world, and the angels do the rest.

If your mind tends to be caught up in the affairs of the day when you are trying to wind down for the night, you might try this "letting-go practice" to ready yourself for sleep and lucid dreaming.

1. Pray for lucid awareness while your body is sleeping.

2. Focus on the gentle beating and loving vibration of your heart.

3. Observe the movement of the breath as you do gentle, deep breathing.

4. Envision yourself enveloped in shimmering white light.

5. Visualize yourself in a beautiful, uplifting nature setting.

6. Review the scenes and emotions of your day with peaceful nonattachment while repeating to yourself, "Life is but a dream."

All of us have times when we want to go on retreat—moments when we want to close the door on the cares of the day and explore the inner secrets of our soul. How about making your next retreat a "lucid dreaming" retreat?

Tibetan Dream Yoga

Lama Tenzin Wangyal Rinpoche teaches the spiritual practice known as Tibetan dream yoga. He tells how when he was a little boy he was always fascinated by dreams, and when he came to the West he realized that dreams were also important in this culture. He wanted to bring the Tibetan way of looking at dreams and understanding them to the West.

Rinpoche says a dream "is important because it is one of the best ways to understand the deepest aspects of ourselves. It is also one of the most important ways to heal."[2] In his view every dream is potentially healing in some way, particularly lucid dreams. The practice of dream yoga includes lucid dreaming as well as other procedures that prepare the dreamer for continuity between waking and sleeping states of consciousness.

The foundation of dream yoga is in the way the mind is used during waking life. How we use our mind when we are awake interacts with what we do when we are sleeping or dreaming. As we change the way we relate to people and events in our waking life, our dream experiences reflect those changes. Thus our dreams are reflections or interpretations of daytime happenings as well as inner messages from our soul or Higher Self.

Rinpoche suggests that we begin to train ourselves in the practice of dream yoga while we are awake. How? By observing and focusing our wandering mind and by harnessing and stabilizing our emotions. We can nurture such stability by being aware of the gifts of life, celebrating our positive experiences and fostering a joyful attitude.

The lama makes the point that as sentient beings we have mind and awareness, and yet we have difficulty controlling our minds when we are in *samsara,* the realm of mortality. He suggests that we develop a method of mental/emotional mastery, so that we are not driven by our emotions. This is reminiscent of Gautama Buddha's teaching of nonattachment to desires through realizing the Four Noble Truths and practicing the Eightfold Path.[3]

I have found it most helpful in stilling my mind and emotions to cultivate a conscious awareness of and nonattachment to desires, as the Buddha taught. I also attune to the higher vibrations of the heart by meditating on the eternal flame of life in the secret chamber of the heart.

During the day, our thoughts can become scattered and we may develop a sense of unrest, but it is important to enter sleep in a state of peace. It is absolutely vital to gain mastery over the wandering mind and unruly emotions that arise in daily life if we wish to seriously pursue dream yoga. Rinpoche suggests prayer and asking for help from guardians, protectors, or angels—whatever higher beings a person may trust.

Foundational Preparations for Dream Yoga

The first dream-yoga preparation is to become aware of the dreamlike nature of life when we are awake. Rinpoche suggests that in our waking hours we consider everything we perceive—what we see, hear, feel, touch and smell—as if it were a dream. Similar to our training for lucid dreaming, we say to ourselves many times throughout the day, "This is all a dream." From the perspective of our soul and our Higher Self, life in samsara, or mortality, *is* but a dream.

The second preparation is to notice our emotional reactions as if they were also a dream. As Rinpoche points out, we do literally "dream them up through a complex interaction of thoughts, images, bodily states, and sensations." He says our emotional reactivity "does not originate 'out there' in objects. It arises, is experienced, and ceases in you."[4]

So when we decide to be aware of our emotional patterns, our grasping or aversion, we practice saying to ourselves, "This desire is a dream. This fear is a dream. This anger is a dream." As we do so, we come to realize that our emotional reactions to earthly happenings are fleeting and without enduring essence, and our tendency toward grasping and avoiding decreases.

In the third preparation we review the events of the day and our reactions to those experiences before we go to sleep. We allow the memories of the day to arise at the same time that we recognize the dreamlike nature of each experience. As we prepare for sleep, we also strengthen our intention that we will be "awake" in our dream.

We make a strong determination that we will know directly and vividly while we are dreaming that we are indeed dreaming. As Rinpoche says, "The intention is like an arrow that awareness can follow during the night, an arrow directed at lucidity in the dream."[5]

The fourth preparation is to review upon awakening any

dream we may have had. We ask ourselves, "Did I dream? Was I aware that I was in the dream?" We write the dream down or speak it into a tape recorder. And rejoice if it was a lucid dream!

As we begin to gain mastery, we take joy in our success in having a lucid experience. When we are not successful, we simply recognize that it takes time and practice—without berating ourselves. And we resolve to put a stronger intention into our practice.

Rinpoche teaches the importance of praying with all of our heart for success. He reminds us that prayer is like a magical power that we all have and forget to use. He suggests that we purify our minds as much as possible before sleep, use whatever skills we have learned to release negative emotions and tension in the body, and consciously choose to generate compassion for ourselves and all life.

Winding Down

We can wind down from our day and purify our minds as Rinpoche advises in any number of ways. We may do devotional reading, prayers, decrees or meditation. We may invoke the light of compassion and the guiding presence of angels, masters and our Higher Self. We can practice a posture of nonattachment toward any unpleasantness of the day and a ritual of forgiveness for anyone who has harmed us or whom we may have harmed or distressed.

We might want to play our favorite musical instrument or listen to uplifting classical music while we take a soothing herbal bath. You could undoubtedly add to the list with your own favorite winding-down, relaxing and inspirational activities.

Rinpoche recommends a special nine purifications breathing exercise to release all obstacles within, such as potentials for illness or impediments from the past. He also teaches a practice of guru yoga, whereby through intense reverence, devotion, and appreciation of the master's wisdom light, we develop a heart connection and oneness of mind with the guru. In the ultimate state of blissful oneness, the guru dissolves into light and enters the heart, residing there as our innermost essence.

The Practices of Dream Yoga

The main procedures of dream yoga, as Rinpoche teaches it, include a practice while falling asleep and practices to be done in three waking periods during the night.

Sleep is broken into roughly two-hour segments. The periods of waking between each of these sleep segments are the "working periods" for dream yoga. In each working period, a particular position is taken, a special type of breathing is performed and the mind is focused on a definite image in a specific chakra.

This is a very specific and detailed yogic practice that is best done under the direction of a Tibetan yoga teacher. You might also wish to purchase the excellent book *The Tibetan Yogas of Dream and Sleep* by Tenzin Wangyal Rinpoche, which fully describes the spiritual practices of dream and sleep yoga.

For people who can't imagine waking up several times

during the night because they already aren't getting enough sleep, we may remember that parents frequently wake up to tend their children during the night and many of us wake up to go to the bathroom and go right back to sleep.

Waking up for dream practice is simply taking another view to waking up during the night. Those who seriously pursue dream yoga often wake up two to three times a night without experiencing any adverse effects.

Dream Yoga's Four Major Tasks

Here is my adaptation of Rinpoche's description of the four major tasks of dream yoga. Please bear in mind that this is a brief outline of a complex series of yogic practices. To do dream yoga as a serious practice, one needs to be guided by a master teacher.

1. **Focusing.** When going to sleep, bring your mind and awareness into a blissful state of peace and centeredness. Lie on your side,* breathe gently and relax the body. Visualize a beautiful four-petaled ruby lotus in your throat chakra. In the center and on each petal is a luminous crystal made of pure light. (Instead of the crystal you may visualize a spiritual symbol that is meaningful to you.) As you enter sleep, focus on the crystal (or the symbol).

   This first practice generates stability and the ability to focus. It assists you to maintain a sense of

*Men lie on their right side, women on their left, with knees bent for stability, the top arm stretched out along the side and the hand of the other arm under the cheek.

peacefulness and restful awareness. In turn, it prepares the way for the succeeding practices that increase clarity and develop inner strength and fearlessness.

2. **Increasing Clarity.** Set your alarm for two hours. When you awaken, take the same side posture. Gently inhale and hold your breath as you visualize the breath rising from the base of the spine to your brow or the third-eye chakra. Gently exhale and completely relax. Repeat this seven times.

   During this practice, the focus is on merging and becoming one with the clarity and luminosity of a brilliant white sphere of light in the third-eye chakra. This practice generates increasing clarity of vision and higher consciousness.

3. **Strengthening Presence.** This practice is performed in the next waking period, approximately two hours after the first one. Lie back with your head on a high pillow and your legs lightly crossed above the ankles. Make sure your body is comfortable while you take twenty-one deep, gentle breaths with full awareness of your breathing.

   The point of focus is the heart chakra. This practice is to develop a sense of one's inner power over thoughts and visions, the strength to be fully aware yet nonreactive when encountering any kind of appearance or circumstance. Thus, the strengthening presence generates a sense of safety and security in all situations.

4. **Developing Fearlessness.** Approximately two hours after the last waking, we practice facing our "wrathful aspect" in order to overcome fear. There is no particular position to take, nor any special breathing exercise. Just get comfortable. The focus is on the darker aspect of the imagination, including wrathful deities and elements that would destroy the image of the self.

This practice is in the service of becoming fearless. The dreamer calls out the inner causes for frightening dreams and thereby begins to transform negative or fear-inducing karmic residue.[6]

Transforming Fearsome Dream Figures

When we work with lucid dreams in dream yoga, we practice challenging and transforming whatever we encounter. As Rinpoche says, "There is no boundary to experience that can't be broken in the dream; we can do whatever occurs to us to do."[7]

This reminds me of an experience that my spiritual teacher Elizabeth Clare Prophet shared with her students. A three-year-old child announced one morning that she had dreamed a devil was chasing her. When her mother asked, "What did you do?" the child replied, "I slapped him, and he went away!" The child took action, and the devil of the mind disappeared. Truly, out of the mouths and actions of babes can come great wisdom and practical solutions.

A friend of mine tells a similar story about a dream her grandson had. The child woke up and said to his mother,

"I had a dream about a giant." When his mother asked what happened, he said, "I was fighting with the giant, but he was so big that I just made myself smaller and smaller. And I flew up and went into his eye. And do you know what was in there? Stars!"[8]

Another dreamer, a young man, had a recurring nightmare where he was being attacked by a large and ferocious grizzly bear. These dreams were very frightening to him. As he started practicing lucid dreaming, one night he decided to gather up his courage and ask the bear what he was doing in his dream and what he wanted. The bear instantly turned into his father, who had been very overbearing and abusive to him as a child.

In his dream, he was able to talk openly with his father and tell him the truth about the pain the father had caused him. At the end of the dream, he forgave his father, and the nightmare never recurred. In addition, he was able to transfer this forgiveness of his father into his waking life.

We know we are making progress when our dreams become more clear and complete, when we remember them, when we have lucid dreams, and ultimately, when we can guide our dreams instead of being at the mercy of our unconscious conflicts and shadow dramas.

Sleep Yoga and the Clear Light

Once you have mastered dream yoga, you are ready to learn the more advanced practice of sleep yoga. In this practice you develop lucid awareness in between the dream experiences. Ask yourself, "Do I have any level of awareness or any way of understanding who I am when I am asleep but not dreaming?"

This is the purpose of sleep yoga—to have full awareness even in the deep-sleep state, where people typically have a complete lack of awareness. Tibetan yogis teach that the deep-sleep state is where we may have "clear light" experiences but that this is a very difficult realization to attain.

Rinpoche describes three kinds of sleep: (1) the state of sleep in which there is no sense of dreaming or consciousness, and we awaken not remembering anything; (2) samsaric sleep, where we have dreams; and (3) clear light sleep.

This clear light sleep is the practice and the goal of sleep yoga. In it we develop *rigpa,* "pure awareness," or "knowing." Rinpoche tells us that in the clear light "there are no qualities ... no time or boundaries. There are no distinctions at all.... In sleep practice, the recognition is not of an object by a subject but is the nondual recognition of pure awareness, the clear light, by awareness itself.... The clear light is like seeing without an eye, an object, or a seer."[9]

The clear light experience is analogous to what happens at death where there is a moment of total dissolution of the subjective self and then images arise in the *bardo,* the intermediate state between death and rebirth.

Preparation and Practice of Sleep Yoga

The same basic preparations are recommended for sleep yoga as are described in dream yoga. At a minimum, focus upon the heart, generate or invoke compassion, and give prayers for clear light sleep.

Some adepts of this practice leave a light on. This helps maintain awareness, because the external light can connect the adept to the luminosity of his or her internal light. It can be a bridge between the world of form and the experience of formlessness. It can also give the mind a support as the adept moves toward pure nondualistic awareness—the goal of sleep yoga.

In sleep yoga the same sleeping-on-the-side position is taken while you visualize four blue lotus petals in your heart chakra. In the center of the petals is a luminous sphere of pure light, which reflects the blue of the lotus petals and becomes a brilliant blue-white. In your one-pointed focus upon it, you become one with the brilliant blue-white light. You are that light as you imagine facing to the east.

On each of the lotus petals is a luminous orb of light. The orb in the front, or east, is yellow; the orb to the left, or north, is green; the orb behind you, to the west, is ruby; and the orb to the right, the south, is blue.

Feel the loving protection of the *dakinis,* feminine deities who are a manifestation of the enlightened mind. Or see masters and angels who are more familiar to you.

Pray for the sleep of clear light instead of the sleep of dreams or the sleep in which you remember nothing. Your strong intention and devotion become an inner power that pierces the veil of ignorance that is masking the realm of the clear light.

As you get comfortable before entering sleep, merge your awareness with the beauty and warmth of the yellow light (on the petal facing outward) to begin the dissolution of your conceptual mind. As your vision decreases and you close your eyes, shift your awareness to the green sphere of light (to the left) and allow your identity to begin to fade. As your senses become more muted, shift awareness to the ruby light (behind you), and then as all senses are fading into nothingness, focus on the blue light (to the right).

At this point, all is quiet; sensory experience is gone. As the body completely enters sleep, awareness will fully merge with the central blue-white sphere. When you are successful, you will have no object of awareness or visualization or location. You are the clear light itself during sleep.

Realize that all of these stages are a gradual lessening of sensory experience. Usually when we go to sleep this is an unconscious process we all go through. What happens in sleep yoga is that we go through this same process while merged with intention and awareness, so there is a gradual unfolding of nonduality, the experience of clear light.

If you wake up in the middle of this process, simply start over again. As in dream yoga, it is best to awaken three times during the night (at approximately two-hour intervals) until your practice is well developed. Each time you awaken, ask yourself, "Did I sleep the sleep of unawareness? Did I dream? Or was I in the clear light, in pure nondualistic awareness?"

Too much expectation may interfere with progress in dream or sleep yoga. The lama explains,

> People expect to have immediate results. You can make instant coffee, but not instant success with dream and sleep yoga.... Also ... you need to have joy about

doing the dream yoga practice. If you think of it as work, that is a very big mistake.... View it as a joyful, relaxing practice, like taking a warm shower or lying in a comfortable bed and finding the right position before we go to sleep....

It is important to remember that the dharma* is really flexible and we need to remain flexible. Do not allow yourself to become trapped by the practice. Experiment. This doesn't mean that you should throw out the tradition and make up your own. These practices are powerful and effective and they have been the vehicle for countless people to realize liberation.

At death you reach the borderline between samsara and nirvana—the intermediate state, the famous bardo. ... If one can integrate with the clear light of sleep then one can integrate with the clear light of death. All the beings who achieved enlightenment and became Buddhas crossed the border and entered the clear light. We, too, with great determination and joyful work, have the capacity to do the same.[10]

---

*In the context of this teaching on dream and sleep yoga, dharma is both the spiritual teachings, which ultimately derive from the Buddhas, and the spiritual path itself.

CHAPTER ELEVEN

Dream Analysis from the Adept's Point of View

To dream the impossible dream,
To reach the unreachable star.

—JOE DARION
The Impossible Dream

Another interesting way of interpreting dreams from a spiritual perspective comes to us from Theosophy. In 1903 C. W. Leadbeater published the book *Dreams: What They Are and How They Are Caused.* In it he discusses not only the physiological aspects of dreaming but also the etheric and astral aspects involved.

Throughout the book Leadbeater refers to the dreamer as the ego. He says the ego may be either spiritually undeveloped or highly developed to the point of being an adept possessing transcendent powers. (Jesus demonstrated such powers when he transformed the water into wine at the wedding in Cana.[1]) In Theosophy the spiritual powers of the adept are called occult powers.

Leadbeater describes the state of sleep: "When a man falls into deep slumber the higher principles in [his] astral vehicle almost invariably withdraw from the body, and hover in its immediate neighborhood. Indeed, it is the process of this withdrawal which we commonly call 'going to sleep.'... The physical body... [is] lying quietly on the bed, while the ego [the dreamer], in its astral body,* floats with equal tranquility just above it."[2]

---

*The astral body equates with the emotional body, the repository of our emotions and our desires. Leadbeater says the astral body is the dreamer's vehicle for soul travel during sleep.

He says that in an entirely undeveloped soul, the astral body is a wreath of mist floating above the sleeping body. The figure within the mist, the ego, is vague, barely recognizable. It is receptive only to coarser and more violent desires and is only able to move a few yards away from the physical body.

During sleep, the undeveloped soul remains as asleep as its body, essentially "blind to the sights and deaf to the voices of its own higher plane."[3]

In a more evolved person, the mist takes an ovoid shape and the figure within the mist more perfectly resembles the physical body beneath it. The astral body's power of locomotion is greater. It can travel considerable distances from the body and bring back definite impressions about places it visits.

The Mind and the Sleep State

Leadbeater says that in the dream state we are unable to grasp an abstract idea unless it is portrayed as a scene in which we are an actor. Thus, an idea of glory might take shape as a glorious being appearing to us, and a concept of hatred might appear as a person exhibiting violent hatred toward us.

He says that thoughts of a particular location in a dream can result in our being transported to that location in our dream imagery. For example, if we are asleep in the United States and have a passing thought about Ireland, we are instantaneously transported to the Ireland we envision. In contrast, if in our waking state we happen to think of Ireland, we are at the same time completely aware that we are in the United States.

He explains that we live, as it were, in an ocean of everyone's thoughts. These constantly impinge upon the higher or etheric part of our brain. If we watch our thoughts closely, we often find they are largely composed of cast-off fragments of other people's thoughts. When we are asleep, the etheric part of our brain is even more at the mercy of other people's thought-currents since our waking ego is not in control.

During the dream state, various segments of time may be compressed into one scene and the past, present and future become the eternal Now. A person might awaken from a dream of having lived through an entire lifetime after being asleep only a few seconds.

As an example of this, Leadbeater relates the story from the Koran about a visit the prophet Muhammad made to heaven one morning. During the visit he saw many different regions of heaven and had a number of lengthy conversations with angels. However, when he returned to his physical body, he discovered that only a few seconds had passed. As the story goes, the water had not yet all run out from a jug he had accidentally overturned when he began his journey to heaven.[4]

Setting Our Consciousness in the Right Direction

If we want to remember what we learn during sleep, then during our waking hours we need to practice attuning our mind to higher consciousness and controlling our thoughts and lower passions. When we practice concentrated thinking in the daytime, the habit carries over into the night.

We train our brain to listen to us as we hold our mind in check and master it in the sense of being continually aware of exactly what we are thinking and why. As a result, it will not respond to the random energies floating around us from other people, and we are more apt to remember the insights we learn from the higher planes.

When we go to sleep at night, Leadbeater instructs us to focus our attention on our aura, the vibrating sheaths of energy that surround us, and to will the outer surface of that aura to become like a shell. The vibratory shell that forms will seal us from passing streams of thoughts.

He also teaches that it is easy to be passive and easily influenced during sleep by the thoughts of others directed to us.

For example, Donna was still asleep at 8:30 A.M. when the answering machine at her office took a message that she needed to make a bank deposit. Meanwhile, she was dreaming that she was making a bank deposit, asleep and not aware of the message on the answering machine. She said, "I was in kind of a dozing state when this happened, awakened shortly afterward and checked my messages because I had overslept. I realized the message and the dream occurred at the same time."

Since we are so receptive to the thoughts and images of other people whose attention is upon us, we need to enter the sleep state focusing our thoughts on high and holy concepts, the loftiest thoughts of which we are capable. As we do so, we will draw similar energies to us. Our rest will be more peaceful, and our mind will be open to the higher impressions and closed to the lower ones. We will have set our consciousness in the right direction.

If we fall asleep with impure and earthly thoughts floating

through our brain, we attract to ourselves the same kind of energy. Then we may be troubled by passions and desires that keep us from the illumined vision and instruction available in the etheric plane. Instead of a high dream, we may actually act out unfulfilled lower desires, having dreams of sexual passions or angry, violent interchanges.

In other words, it is our state of consciousness when we enter sleep that determines where our soul resides during sleep. As the Bible puts it, "Let not the sun go down upon your wrath."[5]

Thus, we are responsible for our thoughts, feelings and actions, whether awake or asleep. According to the great law of karma, whatever we send out returns to us. We make karma, therefore, when we are asleep as well as when we are awake. Of course, the more we learn to control our thoughts and feelings in the waking state, the more we will be able to control them when asleep.

Ultimately, we can learn to go beyond dreaming, as we've seen in the Tibetan practices of dream and sleep yoga. The adepts have taught that we can leave our body in full conscious awareness and simply step into the higher planes of existence. Leadbeater summarizes this teaching:

> If one guides his soul persistently upward, its inner senses will at last begin to unfold; the light within the shrine will burn brighter and brighter, until at last the full continuous consciousness comes, and then he will dream no more.
>
> To lie down to sleep will no longer mean for him to

sink into oblivion, but simply to step forth radiant, rejoicing, strong, into that fuller, nobler life where fatigue can never come—where the soul is always learning, even though all his time be spent in service; for the service is that of the great Masters of Wisdom, and the glorious task They set before him is to help ever to the fullest limit of his power in Their never-ceasing work for the aiding and the guidance of the evolution of humanity.[6]

Teachings of a Twentieth-Century Prophet

I have learned a great deal about the adepts' views of dreams from my spiritual teacher Elizabeth Clare Prophet. She suggests we write down our dreams as soon as we awaken so that we will not lose the memory and symbolic meaning for the soul. She explains that our soul may be portrayed by another character in our dreams. That character may represent a level of soul consciousness that our outer mind does not fully comprehend.

Our soul may be trying to share an understanding or convey a lesson to us. We may also learn in our dreams how we relate to our soul, because the soul often appears as a child in the dream. The way we act toward that child may in fact be what our real relationship is to our own soul.

Mrs. Prophet teaches that the dream state is a series of experiences of the soul. Some people's souls are quickened. Other people's souls are in a sphere of their mental body, which causes them to be very concrete in their outlook on life. They are not in contact with their soul's inner experiences and consequently may not even have dream recollections.

She also tells us some dreams are a private experience between the dreamer and the dreamer's higher mind and soul. Others are an out-of-the-body experience with other people and the spiritual masters.

One of Mrs. Prophet's students reported a dream in which he was in a gigantic place of large hallways and big rooms with people moving all over the place. He had a meeting with someone there. As he was on the way out of this meeting room, he was walking down the hallway and thought, "I wonder if Maureen is here."

As he was going into one of the meeting rooms, suddenly Maureen came out. They held hands as they walked, and it was the most exhilarating feeling he had ever had in his life. He woke up crying.

Then he dreamed again that he had that feeling of walking with Maureen. About two weeks later he saw an almost identical-looking person in a classroom of the college he attends. She left and he never encountered her again. He asked Mrs. Prophet what she thought of this experience.

She responded that when people have been on the spiritual path for a while and have such dreams, they are often remembering a visit to an etheric retreat. They are in the halls of the Great White Brotherhood.*

In general, such dreams, especially when a person has the deep feelings upon awakening that he was describing, are an expression of relief and emotion for the inner encounter. The

---

*The Great White Brotherhood is a spiritual order of Western saints and Eastern adepts. "White" refers to the aura of white light that surrounds these spiritual beings. See page 235 endnote 15 for more information.

dream is a way of thinning the veil whereby we remember what we are doing at inner levels.

She told this young man that there is a great probability that the person he met at the college is the person he met in the inner temple. There are no accidents in the universe. She counseled him to pursue his spiritual path with all his heart because the union of his soul with his Higher Self would be the magnet of the relationship.

She said, "If it is intended for your paths to cross again, they will. But if you suddenly start running all over the city looking for this person, you can get off on the wrong track and actually lose her when in fact, through God, it might be a very simple drawing together."

She suggested he put the situation in his prayers for the will of God and the protection of the work he is pursuing at inner levels. She reminded him that the light he is carrying is the magnet that will create the encounter if it is meant to happen.[7]

Journeying at Night Takes Us through Many Levels

At times Elizabeth Clare Prophet has also given teaching on the soul's nightly journeying. She once explained:

The journeying at night takes us through many levels. What you eat before you retire may affect how you sleep, your dream state and the kind of dreams you have. Other influences may include such things as the temperature of the room, proper air flow or the proximity to other people whose vibrations may be different.

When you retire, you hope you are leaving your physical body and going forth. But sometimes due to the tensions and pressures of life, we stay very close to our bodies. Sometimes when the body is in danger, we stay close. In the process of being close to home, we may not get any farther out of the physical body than into the astral body, particularly when we have difficulties in sleeping.

On the other hand, you may be journeying in the etheric, but the journey is like a knife passing through a cake—sometimes it comes out clean and sometimes it has a little cake and icing on it after it has passed through. And so, when you pass through the different planes, you pick up impressions of those planes, and that is what may be quivering or vibrating on the portion of us that dreams—the residue of passing through.

You may go into the etheric octave and be in a very deep sleep where you are having experiences at inner levels. But you may return and pass through the cities, pass through the earth. You may pass through the levels of your own soul's evolution, where a tea party may not be an actual tea party but a symbolical way in which your Christ Self, your Higher Self, is teaching your soul a lesson.

There are all kinds of dreams. And one way of looking at them is to understand that a character in the dream may represent your soul. Most often that character isn't you, it's someone else in the dream. By objectively observing this other character, you may be observing something happening to your soul that your Higher Self wants you to know.

So, it could be an astral kind of a dream. It could be

a chase. It could be all kinds of topsy-turvy, Alice-in-Wonderland things. But there's a thread running through it. Your conscious mind is not ready to accept the lesson, so in the dream state the lesson comes through the subconscious, which has no barriers to incongruities. When you wake up, if you write down this dream, you may receive the interpretation of it.

Now, I had an interesting dream once in which I figured myself with a young child. I was in the ocean with this child, and she fell down in the water and was drowning. She was going deeper and deeper into the water, and I dived after her and saved her from drowning.

The lesson of the dream was that the child was my own soul, and my own soul was drowning in a particular circumstance that I was allowing to continue in my life. My interpretation of the dream was that I, in the person of my Christ Self and my conscious mind, would go after and save my own soul. I would see to it that my soul was not left to drown in an unjust and insupportable circumstance.

I came to the realization one day, when this whole situation was through, that while I had been trying to save another soul, it was my own soul that could have been lost. And so, I realized that my soul had been saved by the love of God and by my own determination of right action.

There are all kinds of situations in dreams. They are actual teachings if you can pull the threads of them together. But the unpleasant things and all kinds of details that make no sense are like the cake on the knife if you've been traveling and are coming back—or even if you never did travel but just hung around the astral plane because of some impurity of your body or mind. All of these things can happen in one night because it doesn't actually take that long to go to an etheric retreat and come back. . . .

There is a conflict of terms in different writings about the astral and etheric planes. In the etheric plane, there is a lower etheric level that contains the perversions of the memory of God, or the records that are not of the light. So you might say there's a lower and a higher etheric plane, and the lower one has a certain correspondence to the astral plane and the astral body. . . .

There's an amazing thing about life—there is no-where you can go and read a rule book that comes up with a perfect answer to every equation. We have all this teaching, and the teaching itself is like input in the com-puter of our Christ consciousness. We have all the vastness of the teaching and certain elements are brought to bear on certain situations.

Because of our divine experience, our ongoing expe-rience of thousands of embodiments of being chelas* of the masters, we have a set of experiences, a set of teach-ings. And then we have a Christ mind, which is infinite. When we meditate on that mind and on the experience and the teaching, we arrive at the best possible way of dealing with a situation.

Sometimes we make a misjudgment or a miscalcula-tion, and we learn by our mistakes. That's the nature of the schoolroom we're in and the nature of free will. But

Chela is a Sanskrit term for a student or disciple of a master.

even that becomes a part of our cosmic computer of divine knowledge. That's our personal gnosis. We're not going to make that mistake again because it was very costly.

So in the mistakes as well as in the victories, we forge our Christhood. That's why it takes time to become Christlike, because you become that by free will and by experience. It just isn't brought down upon you like some kind of a machine that is superimposed upon you and all of a sudden you're there.[8]

On another occasion a student asked Mrs. Prophet about nightmares. She replied:

Some dreams are recollections of experiences in the temples of light. They will be very high. They will be full of light.

You may remember an experience of being in a classroom studying. This means that as you were leaving your body, your soul rose into your etheric envelope. And in your etheric envelope, you slid right through the astral plane and the mental plane to get into the etheric level, where the masters' retreats are.

Now, astral nightmares are a different matter. If you don't have your protection on or if you've had an argument or discord in your house before you go to bed, then when you are leaving your body, you kind of get caught in the astral. You don't slide through with your energy field of protection. You get caught there and you start dreaming about the astral plane or episodes in your own astral body that are coming to the fore.

Now another circumstance of dreams may be that you get out just fine. You go up to the masters' retreats. Around five or six in the morning, you come back to your body. But as you return, you don't get through the astral debris. Just before you reach your physical consciousness, you bump into the astral mire and have one of those nightmare dreams that occur just before you wake up in the morning.[9]

The astral plane, then, is where you have the bad dreams, and the etheric plane is where you have visions and memories of high experiences.[10]

Mark Prophet, Elizabeth's late husband and ascended twin flame, was also a pioneering spiritual leader. He once made this comment about out-of-the-body experiences:

Quite a few people have told us of dreams where they were flying. This is a subconscious memory that often functions for two reasons. One, because there was a time when humanity knew how to fly physically. Those of you familiar with the story of the great yogi Milarepa recall how he used to pass across the sky and people would say, "There goes that crazy yogi Milarepa again."

We've lost the art of flying. We're not birds; we're very much earthbound. But some people travel in their finer bodies—they "fly" in that way. And so these two memories of flying are within us.[11]

Nicholas Roerich and the Mystical Symbology of Dreams

Nicholas Roerich was a prolific artist, writer, educator, explorer, philosopher, cultural humanitarian and peacemaker. He was nominated for the Nobel Peace Prize in 1929 and 1935 for his efforts to promote international peace and to protect art treasures in time of war.

Roerich was a spiritual devotee connected with the Theosophical Society and according to some of his followers had contact with Morya and Koot Hoomi, renowned Mahatmas of the East. He had respect for the esoteric meaning of dreams and included two of them in his book *Shambhala: In Search of the New Era.*

As Elizabeth Clare Prophet explains in *The Lost Years of Jesus,* Roerich was revered worldwide in his time, not only for the esoteric knowledge and mystical understanding he had but also for the illumined, beneficent presence of the man himself. She writes:

> Biographers have written a great deal about all phases of Roerich's life except one: the capstone of his endeavors, the force which gave direction, unity, and meaning to his multiple activities—his spiritual life.
>
> Somewhere along the line, the Roerichs acquired a profound understanding of the literature and traditions of esoteric religion—especially esoteric Buddhism.
>
> No doubt Nicholas Roerich's intimate knowledge of the ways of the East, combined with his diverse experience and great learning, explains why he was received

with honor almost everywhere he went on his first Central Asia expedition, why the Chinese marveled at his learning and referred to him as "the Initiate," and why the Mongolians reportedly said, "Such great universal personalities as Roerich are walking the path of the Bodhisattvas of the highest order as absolute lights of the century.... Therefore, our country considers the visit of Professor Roerich ... a great honor and a joy."[12]

In *Shambhala,* published in 1930, Roerich relates two dreams replete with mystical symbols. They were very likely prompted by World War I (1914–1918) and were possibly a prophecy of World War II yet to come. To this advocate of peace and humanitarianism, such wars must surely have been anathema.

Mrs. Prophet read Roerich's dreams to her students:

> Such were the dreams before the war: We were traveling through a field. Behind the hill the clouds rose. A storm. Through a cloud, head downwards, a fiery serpent pierced the earth. The serpent was double-headed.

> Or another dream: Again we travel over a gray plain. No sign of life. Before us, a high hill glimmers dark. We look, but it is not a hill; it is a huge, coiled gray serpent.

> And long before were conjurations. The evil ones were conjured. The untruth was conjured. Bird and beast were conjured. Earth and water were conjured. But to no avail. The monsters crept out.

> Later were signs. They did not perceive them. They did not trust them. They did not grasp them. The crowds stamped upon them.

And the serpent awoke. The enemy of mankind rose. Attempted by slander to conquer the world. To destroy cities. To defame temples. Turn to ashes human strivings.

He rose to his own destruction.

There were conjurations. There were signs.

Dreams remained. Those dreams that are fulfilled.

He laid himself to rest for the night.

He thought—I shall see great Magi.

There was desire to see—how they look.

There was desire to hear—what names they bear.

He wished to see what is bound to their saddles. What road they take. They should reveal. Whence and whither.

But they did not appear, the Magi.

Possibly it was too soon.

Did not start out yet.

Instead of the Magi two others appeared.

One middle-aged in an old blue shirt. In an old dark kaftan. Long hair. In the right hand three staffs.

He holds them today with points upwards. Mark, upwards. All has its meaning. But this is Saint Prokopyi, himself.

He who saved Ustyng the Great.

He, who took away the stony cloud from the city. He, who upon high shores prayed for the unknown travelers.

Marvelous tidings! Himself came Prokopyi the righteous.

And another one with Him—white and old. In one hand a sword and in another the city.

Certainly he is Saint Nicholas.

Instead of the Magi with the star, these came.

Prokopyi speaks:

"Do not depart from the earth. The earth is red, red hot with evil. But the heat of evil nurtures the roots of the Tree. And upon this Tree the good creates its Benevolent nest. Attain the labor on earth. Ascend to the heavenly ocean, the resplendent, but dark only for us. Guard the Benevolent Tree. Good lives on it. The earth is the source of sorrow, but out of sorrow grow joys. He who is the highest knows the predestined date of your joy.

"Do not depart from the earth. Let us sit down and ponder about far-off wanderers."

The other, the white one, lifted the sword.

And people came closer to him. Many came forward.

"Nicholas, the Gracious! Thou Miracle Maker! Thou, All-powerful! Thou, Holy Warrior! Thou, Conqueror of Hearts! Thou, Leader of true thoughts, Thou, Knowing heavenly and earthly forces!

"Thou, Guardian of the Sword! Thou, Protector of Cities! Thou knowing the Truth! Do you hear the prayers, Mighty One!

"Evil forces are battling against us.

"Protect, Thou Mighty One, the Holy City! The resplendent city calls wrath in the enemy. Accept, Thou Mighty One, the beautiful city. Raise, Father, the Sacred Sword! Invoke, Father, all saintly warriors. Miracle-maker, manifest a stern face! Cover the cities with the holy sword! Thou canst, to Thee is given Power!

"We stand without fear and tremor...."[13]

Mrs. Prophet commented on these mystical dreams:

Roerich's conveyance of dreams containing mystical symbols is done in the way we experience dreams. They are cryptic. They are expressed in very short sentences or groups of words that are not full sentences. It is Zen and Oriental. It reflects the type of writing that El Morya does because Nicholas Roerich is the chela of El Morya.[14]

It's a stream-of-consciousness writing. You have to read it about three times to begin to realize the flow. The reason he wrote it that way is because in his dreams he was in and out of both the astral plane (with the signs of the serpents and the monsters) and the etheric plane (the biding place of the saints).

In his dream he calls out for help, and he hears the people calling out for help to Saint Nicholas, to the one who is given power. And finally, there is the affirmation within the dream of the rock of identity, "We stand without fear and tremor."

So having experienced the terror of the dream—the testing, the apparition of the saint, not seeing the Magi but yet seeing them—one then affirms one's position in the physical octave: "We stand without fear and tremor, but thou, O God, through thy saint, hear us." In the dream there is a call to the saint as Father: "Manifest a stern face!" (to the enemy, of course). "Cover the cities with the holy sword! ... Invoke, Father, all saintly warriors."

Even in the dream state—waking or sleeping dream state—we have the awareness that our being interpenetrates many levels of consciousness, and we have the awareness that we need help. The sense of the need for help, the necessity of the *need* for divine intervention, is the very reason for the formation of the Great White Brotherhood[15]—because that intercession, that help, must be organized.

You can imagine yourself as an ascended master looking upon clusters of chelas around the world who are not yet fortified by having come together. They are like isolated pools of water.

In this movement we have a great uniting of forces. But there are many other streams, rivulets, ponds, if you will, of groups in the light who are facing Antichrist and calling for help. The Brotherhood would see our strength in union.[16]

CHAPTER TWELVE

Nicholas Roerich's Dreams: A Message for Our Soul

The heat of evil nurtures the roots of the Tree. And upon this Tree the good creates its Benevolent nest.

—NICHOLAS ROERICH
Shambhala

As we look at Nicholas Roerich's dreams recorded in his book *Shambhala,* we realize that in addition to their esoteric significance for his time they can be a teaching to the soul of each of us today. This is undoubtedly why Roerich wrote them down for posterity to contemplate.

The interpretation that follows evolves out of my understanding of spiritual and psychological principles as well as the time period and culture represented in the dreams. Someone else might interpret the dreams differently.

We may also wish to view the dreams as if they were our souls' nightmare adventures to see what we can learn about personal and cultural shadow elements.

A Time of Inner Troubles

Such were the dreams before the war: We were traveling through a field. Behind the hill the clouds rose. A storm. Through a cloud, head downwards, a fiery serpent pierced the earth. The serpent was double-headed.

This first dream glyph forecasts war or a time of inner troubles, what we might call a warring of the members in our inner world. Thus our soul travels through a field, or an earthly level of consciousness. The hill we see represents a higher consciousness or some kind of height to which we have attained. Yet storm clouds signal trouble ahead.

The fiery serpent plunging headfirst through the cloud to pierce the earth could easily represent humanity's collective negativity. This consciousness, moving through the storm clouds of our mind, can pierce and poison our earthly self. As a double-headed serpent, it has a double amount of virulence. It might also symbolize double-mindedness or even the "poison" of duality.

We learn from this brief dream glyph to be ever vigilant in the protection of our personal consciousness from mass thoughts interpenetrating our minds. I believe it is even more necessary today than it was in Roerich's day because of the increase of destructive activities everywhere.

For example, in the early 1900s, drugs, sexual perversion and violent entertainment were not as much a part of the mass consciousness as they are today. Today, because of the magnification of destructive forces, people are more vulnerable to acting them out.

This is what we see in large crowds of people at political rallies, sports events or rock concerts when emotions run high. Such a crowd can go beyond being a wildly enthusiastic audience to becoming a threatening mob. Ordinary people in such situations do and say things they normally would never dream of doing or saying.

Expand this drama to the global level through mass media and telecommunications and we see how we are all subject to the influence of the mass consciousness. On an energetic level, we encounter the conglomerate consciousness, benign or virulent, of every major happening on the planet.

Since thoughts of the masses affect individuals, the poisonous double-headed fiery serpent of Roerich's dream can indeed "pierce the earth," essentially piercing the protective shield of the aura and impacting our mental, emotional and physical well-being.

What can we do about it? We can become the guard at the gate of our own consciousness. We can protect ourselves from collective, destructive mind-sets by our inner spiritual commitment, a deep love and respect for life, gentleness of heart and a willingness to stand up for what we believe—in a peaceful way.

We can become peaceful warriors of truth. The serpent mind has no power over the adept of truth.

Conjuring Up Dark Aspects of Consciousness

> Or another dream: Again we travel over a gray plain. No sign of life. Before us, a high hill glimmers dark. We look, but it is not a hill; it is a huge, coiled gray serpent.

In this second dream, similar to the first, the serpents continue to signify the serpentine consciousness, the poisonous deceptive mind that is the enemy of the soul's oneness with God. Traveling over a gray plain with no sign of life symbolizes our unenlightened, earthly consciousness.

The high hill glimmering dark, which is actually a huge coiled gray serpent, indicates the danger, even for a split second, of confusing our higher consciousness with the false high of the dark, serpentine logic and its glitter of false promises.

> And long before were conjurations. The evil ones were
> conjured. The untruth was conjured. Bird and beast were
> conjured. Earth and water were conjured. But to no avail.

For Nicholas Roerich *evil* carried the esoteric understanding of *e-veil,* or energy veil, meaning universal energy used to form a veil of "unreal" energy patterns. This is darkness or unreality in contrast to God's light and reality. Thus, the "evil ones conjured" signify unreal or dark aspects of our own consciousness.

Conjuration means "a solemn invocation" or "a summoning by magic." In this case it means invoking inner forces of creation—for good or for ill. Thus, our dark conjurations represent aspects of our subconscious or unconscious that we need to consciously examine: the evil within, the untruths we have pronounced, the bird and beast, earth and water aspects of ourselves.

We might ask ourselves, "What do these symbols represent within us? What are we allowing to reside within us 'to no avail,' meaning to no benefit or good?"

If we take a good look, we can bring to light those aspects of inner darkness that we would redeem. We can transform our evil into good, our untruth into truth. We can transform our inner birds into doves of peace and our beasts into a lion lying down with the lamb. We can choose to be grounded, down to earth, yet fluid, flexible in our consciousness.

Think of how the symbology of Roerich's dreams might translate into a meaningful insight for you—and help you understand and redeem your own dark side.

Inner Monsters of Illusion

The monsters crept out.

Later were signs. They did not perceive them. They did not trust them. They did not grasp them. The crowds stamped upon them.

Although our conscious intention may be benign, whatever unconscious forces of evil we allow to breed within us can take over. Thus, in the dream, "the monsters crept out."

What does that mean for each of us? How do the monsters within—monsters of illusion or destructiveness or negativity—manage to creep out of the unconscious realm and take us over when our conscious intent is to be positive, constructive and real? Even the apostle Paul noted the problem: "The good that I would, I do not: but the evil which I would not, that I do."[1]

In experiencing Roerich's dream as our own, we realize that such monsters are unredeemed aspects of ourselves coming to the surface of awareness. But even though these signs of inner troubles appear, we do not necessarily realize there is a problem. We have internalized the negative conglomerate of the mass consciousness and therefore are numb to the dark side.

In hindsight, will we have to say that we ignored the inner signs, that we "stamped upon them?" Or will we be able to say with the Buddha, "I AM awake! Mara has no power over me!"*

---

*Mara was the devil-tempter who tempted Gautama prior to his enlightenment under the Bodhi tree. In Buddhism, Mara personifies the conglomerate of evil that each adept must defeat by meditating upon and merging with the Good of the Infinite One.

And the serpent awoke. The enemy of mankind rose. Attempted by slander to conquer the world. To destroy cities. To defame temples. Turn to ashes human strivings.

He rose to his own destruction.

There were conjurations. There were signs.

The awakening of the serpent, the enemy of soul and Spirit, signifies the awakening of the deceptive, slanderous, serpentine mind. This mind attempts to conquer our personal world, to destroy the city of our being, to defame our inner temple, to turn to ashes our human strivings.

Will we allow it? Will we rise to our own destruction? Or will we determine to dig out, release and redeem those elusive shadow elements?

Awareness of these elements is the first step. Calling to our Higher Self and the angels to help us is the second. Surrendering and allowing all that is not of the light to be stripped from us is the third.

This process of surrendering and being stripped of our negative elements can be understood as the spiritual initiation of the Dark Night of the Soul.[2]

Only when we fully embrace our divine destiny and place our hand in the hand of our guardian angels and Higher Self do we move with a sense of love, gratitude and peace through this initiation—being stripped of all that is dark, worldly or unreal.

We have the example of mystics and saints throughout history. They maintained a one-pointed focus on the loving presence of the Infinite One and they loved their soul. When we determine to be true to our self as a son or daughter of God and to love our self as God loves us, the serpent consciousness has no power over us.

Dreams remained. Those dreams that are fulfilled.

As Roerich's dream tells us, after the conjurations and signs, what will remain are dreams that are fulfilled. What are those dreams? They are the dreams of our soul united with Spirit. No longer dreams, they are soul attainment.

We Will See Great Magi

He laid himself to rest for the night.
He thought—I shall see great Magi.
There was desire to see—how they look.
There was desire to hear—what names they bear.
He wished to see what is bound to their saddles.
What road they take. They should reveal. Whence and whither.
But they did not appear, the Magi.
Possibly it was too soon.
Did not start out yet.

As he lays himself to rest for the night, the dreamer (who is each one of us) thinks, "I shall see great Magi." We, too, may set ourselves to see the three wise men, the Magi, the great masters of divine love, wisdom and power, in our dreams. Perhaps, we, too, may be surprised when, instead of the Magi, two saints appear.

Saint Prokopyi

Instead of the Magi two others appeared.

One middle-aged in an old blue shirt. In an old dark kaftan. Long hair. In the right hand three staffs.

He holds them today with points upwards. Mark, upwards. All has its meaning. But this is Saint Prokopyi, himself.

He who saved Ustyng the Great.

He, who took away the stony cloud from the city. He, who upon high shores prayed for the unknown travelers.

Marvelous tidings! Himself came Prokopyi the righteous.

And another one with Him—white and old. In one hand a sword and in another the city.

Certainly he is Saint Nicholas.

Instead of the Magi with the star, these came.

First comes Saint Prokopyi, representing our Higher Self as a mighty spiritual conqueror. He holds three staffs, which could well represent the powers of our inner Magi—our attainment in divine love, wisdom and power.

These manifest as the sacred threefold flame of life burning brightly upon the altar in the secret chamber of our heart. Holding the staffs upward symbolizes our Higher Self consecrating our attainment to the Eternal Spirit.

Our inner Prokopyi wears the kaftan, the garment of the Eastern adepts, and has long hair, symbolizing our attainment at the level of the Higher Self.

Do Not Depart the Earth

Prokopyi speaks:

"Do not depart from the earth. The earth is red, red hot with evil. But the heat of evil nurtures the roots of the Tree. And upon this Tree the good creates its Benevolent nest."

Prokopyi tells the rest of our inner cast of characters, elements of our soul, not to depart from the earth. In other words, it is not yet our soul's time to ascend to heavenly realms. He reminds us that the earth, or earthly self, is red hot with evil, the energy veil, but that the heat of evil nurtures the roots of benevolence.

I believe this is as true today as it was when Roerich recorded this dream. As we reflect upon the aftermath of evil, the consequences of our negative sowings, we begin to wake up to the tremendous need we have to bend the knee to our God and to redeem ourselves.

We can decide to ask for and to extend forgiveness—and change our ways. We can renew our dedication to take the high road in life and to offer compassion and benevolence to all we meet.

There are markings along the way. We discover footprints of adepts who have gone before us: Moses, who left the riches of Egypt to follow his humble Jewish heritage; Saul of Tarsus, who left behind his carnal nature to become Saint Paul; Prince Siddhartha, who walked away from a human kingdom to become the Buddha.[3]

Many men and women have lived a life of compassion and

benevolence. What will be the destiny of the children of Earth who follow our footprints in the sands of time?

Guard the Benevolent Tree

"Attain the labor on earth. Ascend to the heavenly ocean, the resplendent, but dark only for us. Guard the Benevolent Tree. Good lives on it."

Saint Prokopyi tells us that upon the Tree of Benevolence, our Good, all the good that we do, is building its "Benevolent nest." He advises us to gain our attainment through our labor on Earth, in other words, while we are still in physical embodiment.

When our attainment on Earth is completed, we may ascend to the heavenly ocean that is "dark only for us." This is puzzling but perhaps could mean that as long as we are still on the earth we retain an element of darkness—that thorn in the side, our shadow self, that keeps us from seeing the ultimate luminescence of the heaven world.

"Dark only for us" could also refer to the unknown. As the apostle Paul said, "For now we see through a glass, darkly; but then face to face: now I know in part; but then shall I know even as also I am known. And now abide faith, hope, charity, these three; but the greatest of these is charity."[4]

It is interesting to note that Paul follows his comment on seeing through a glass darkly with the affirmation of faith, hope and charity, the inner gifts of the Magi to the Christ child. We may envision our own soul as a Christ child aborning in the manger of our heart.

Let us reflect on Prokopyi's words to "guard the Benevolent Tree. Good lives on it." This teaching is similar to the Kabbalistic teaching that we must guard the Tree of Life within, meaning to guard the light of the sefirot in our chakras.[5] We may ask ourselves, "Am I guarding the light of the Infinite One shining through the windows of my body temple? If not, why not?"

As we answer such questions and put our answers to work in our lives, we increase in light and understanding and are more likely to experience the etheric nature of our being in our dreams.

Out of Sorrow Grows Joy

"The earth is the source of sorrow, but out of sorrow grow joys. He who is the highest knows the predestined date of your joy."

Truly, as Saint Prokopyi tells us, the earth is the source of sorrow, but out of sorrow grows joy. We can imagine receiving this dream and accepting the teaching to learn from the sorrows and celebrate the joys of life on Earth. The teaching also reminds us that we have a timetable for our soul's return to the higher octaves in the bliss and joy of the ascension, our reunion with Spirit.[6]

"Do not depart from the earth. Let us sit down and ponder about far-off wanderers."

Each of us may also benefit by realizing that Saint Prokopyi emphasizes his warning not to depart from the earth before our time by saying it twice, at the beginning of his speech and now at the ending. This instruction is underlined by the teaching that immediately follows—to "ponder about far-off wanderers," which we can understand as parts of ourselves that have wandered away from the road to divine destiny.

We redeem the inner monsters through correcting our illusions and claiming right motive, right thought, right word and right deed. When we do this, we bring forth the gifts of benevolence, wisdom, compassion, and we care for our soul and for one another the way our Creator cares for us.

Invoking Spiritual Warriors to Stand with Us

The other, the white one, lifted the sword.

And people came closer to him. Many came forward.

"Nicholas, the Gracious! Thou Miracle Maker! Thou, All-powerful! Thou, Holy Warrior! Thou, Conqueror of Hearts! Thou, Leader of true thoughts, Thou, Knowing heavenly and earthly forces!

"Thou, Guardian of the Sword! Thou, Protector of Cities! Thou knowing the Truth! Do you hear the prayers, Mighty One!

"Evil forces are battling against us.

"Protect, Thou Mighty One, the Holy City! The resplendent city calls wrath in the enemy. Accept, Thou Mighty One, the beautiful city. Raise, Father, the Sacred Sword! Invoke, Father, all saintly warriors. Miracle-maker, manifest a stern face! Cover the cities with the holy sword! Thou canst, to Thee is given Power!"

With Saint Prokopyi also comes Saint Nicholas, whose name Roerich bore. We, too, may feel a special closeness to

Saint Nicholas and herald his appearance. Or this divine apparition in our dream might be a different saint whose name and path to sainthood best represent our own sacred walk with God.

The crowd heralding Saint Nicholas represents many parts of our self heralding the divine consciousness that he embodies and imploring the saint to hear our prayers for victory over the inner intruders of evil.

We may make this our own ritual of adoration and prayer. We may ask Saint Nicholas (or our own special saint or Higher Self) to protect our holy city, to protect our resplendent inner city of light, which evokes the wrath of the inner enemy and all of the darkness that opposes the light.

We, too, may ask the saint to raise the sacred sword on our behalf, meaning to wield the power of the sacred word in prayers and fiats* on our behalf.

When we invoke the saints as spiritual warriors to assist us, we begin the process of transforming our inner sense of unreality, our darkness. As the light shines upon our shady motives, miserable feelings, shadowy flaws and shortcomings, they gradually melt away into nothingness.

We do our part when we take courage to do for ourselves exactly what we are asking the saints and our Higher Self to do for us. We do our part when we claim the virtues of our Higher Self to replace those unreal aspects of being. It becomes a divine partnership.

---

*Fiats are short, dynamic statements, exclamations of divine power, wisdom and love, affirmed and accepted in the here and now. They usually begin with the words I AM, meaning "God in me is."

The Stance of the Soul of Light

"We stand without fear and tremor. . . . "

So we choose to take the high road. We pray for courage. We look to the guidance of the saints and masters who have gone before us. We commit ourselves to take the necessary stance for our soul's victory. Thus, we stand without fear or tremor.

This is the stance of the soul of light, for our God is the sure defense in times of trouble. Ultimately, we, too, like Nicholas Roerich, are destined to become victorious adepts of light and love.

Waking or sleeping, then, life is a process of soul initiation and self-transcendence. We move forward when we seek to learn the lessons of our earthly experiences as revealed in our dreams— to pass the tests of divine love and to understand the secrets of our soul and the promptings of angels and our Higher Self.

By so doing we move ever closer to envisioning and becoming the fullness of who we were created to be. We move ever closer to our soul's ultimate destiny in the octaves of light and eternal reality.

In the words of the ascended master Serapis Bey, "It is the very nature of the soul ever to transcend itself as veil after veil of misqualification drops and reveals the transcendent light, [the light] streaming from out the very heart of the Eternal Father into the heart of the Son—the one who is the real you."[7]

Notes

Prologue

1. See the section on "Transpersonal Psychology" in Raymond J. Corsini and Alan J. Auerbach, *Concise Encyclopedia of Psychology,* 2nd ed., abr. (New York: John Wiley & Sons, 1998), pp. 902–3.

Introduction

1. See Tom Brown, Jr., *Grandfather* (New York: Berkley Publishing Group, Berkley Books, 1993).

2. *Heart* (New York: Agni Yoga Society, 1975), pp. 224, 225.

Chapter One: *Mystical Roots of Dream Interpretation*

1. The material in this section includes a compilation of historical information from M.-L. von Franz, "The Process of Individuation," in *Man and His Symbols,* by Carl G. Jung et al. (Garden City, N.Y.: Doubleday & Company, 1964), pp. 161–71, 207–15; and Scott Cunningham, *Dreaming the Divine: Techniques for Sacred Sleep* (St. Paul, Minn.: Llewellyn Publications, 1999), pp. 90–114.

2. Manly P. Hall, *The Secret Teachings of All Ages* (Los Angeles: Philosophical Research Society, 1977), p. CXCIII.

3. Von Franz, "The Process of Individuation," p. 207.

Chapter Two: *Ancient Records and the Scientific View*

1. See Samuel Noah Kramer, *The Sumerians: Their History, Culture, and Character* (Chicago: University of Chicago Press, 1963), pp. 33, 136.

2. Michel Soymié, "Les songes et leur interprétation en Chine," in *Les songes et leur interprétations: Sources orientales* (Paris: Seuil, 1959), p. 284.

3. Description of dream practices in ancient Greece is derived from the writings of Clara E. Hill, *Working with Dreams in Psychotherapy* (New York: Guilford Press, 1996), chapter 3; and Morton T. Kelsey, *God, Dreams, and Revelation,* rev. ed. (Minneapolis, Minn.: Augsburg Fortress, 1991), chapter 3.

4. Gen. 20:2–7.

5. Gen. 37, 39–42.

6. Matt. 2:12, 13.

7. Matt. 27:19.

8. Kelsey, *God, Dreams, and Revelation,* p. 109.

9. The material on the early Christian Church's influence on public opinion about dreams is summarized from Hill, *Working with Dreams in Psychotherapy,* chapter 3; and Kelsey, *God, Dreams, and Revelation,* chapters 5–7.

10. Kelsey, *God, Dreams, and Revelation,* p. 156.

11. The Babylonian Talmud is the authoritative body of Jewish tradition. It was compiled over seven centuries and completed around A.D. 500.

12. *The Chronicle of Elis Gruffydd,* a sixteenth-century manuscript now in the National Library of Wales (MS 5276D), as referenced by Mary Devlin in "The Secret Language of Dreams," *Dell Horoscope,* March 2000, p. 21.

Chapter Three: *Physiology of Sleeping and Dreaming*

1. Summarized from Hill, *Working with Dreams in Psychotherapy,* pp. 11–12.

2. See Wilda B. Tanner, *The Mystical, Magical, Marvelous World of Dreams* (Tahlequah, Okla.: Sparrow Hawk Press, 1988), pp. 12–13.

3. See Piero Ferrucci, *What We May Be: Techniques for Psychological and Spiritual Growth* (Los Angeles: J. P. Tarcher, 1982), pp. 43–44.

4. Tanner, *The Mystical, Magical, Marvelous World of Dreams,* pp. 14–15.

5. See Dr. William Dement, *Some Must Watch While Some Must Sleep* (San Francisco: San Francisco Book Co., 1976).

6. Summary of research findings of Trinder & Kramer, 1971; Koulack & Goodenough, 1976; Carrington, 1972; Winget, Kramer, & Whitman, 1972; Cann & Donderi, 1986; Cartwright, 1977; A. B. Hill, 1974; Lewis, Goodenough, Shapiro & Sleser, 1966; Wallach, 1963. For more details of this research, see Hill, *Working with Dreams in Psychotherapy,* pp. 18–19.

7. See dream research of C. S. Hall and R. L. Van de Castle, *The Content Analysis of Dreams* (New York: Appleton-Century Crofts, 1966); also see Calvin S. Hall's summary of dream research in Raymond J. Corsini and Alan J. Auerbach, *Concise Encyclopedia of Psychology,* 2nd ed., abr., pp. 237–38.

Chapter Four: *Interpreting Symbols and Metaphors*

1. Swiss psychiatrist Carl Jung's shadow archetype is his way of describing the outcropping of our base instincts—the dark side of our human nature. It is the emergence of troubling parts of ourselves, negative traits that we consider forbidden, shameful or taboo. In dreams and myths, the shadow appears as the same sex as the dreamer. Paradoxically, the shadow is both the potential for evil and the potential for good if we embrace the opportunity for transformation and redemption. For an in-depth analysis of the shadow archetype, see *Romancing the Shadow: Illuminating the Dark Side of the Soul,* by Connie Zweig, Ph.D., and Steve Wolf, Ph.D. (New York: Ballantine Books, 1997).

2. For further elaboration of the inner dance of the anima and animus, see my book *Sacred Psychology of Love: The Quest for Relationships That Unite Heart and Soul* (Corwin Springs, Mont.: Summit University Press, 1999), pp. 107–46.

Chapter Five: *Dreams and Visions of Soul and Spirit*

1. Hugh Lynn Cayce et al., *Dreams: The Language of the Unconscious* (Virginia Beach, Va.: A.R.E. Press, 1971), reading 364-4, pp. 5–6.

2. See Elizabeth Clare Prophet with Patricia R. Spadaro, *The Art of Practical Spirituality: How to Bring More Passion, Creativity and Balance into Everyday Life* (Corwin Springs, Mont.: Summit University Press, 2000), p. 52.

3. *Astral* refers to the astral plane, a frequency of time and space beyond the physical, corresponding to the emotional body and the collective unconscious of humanity. Because the astral plane has been muddied by impure thoughts and feelings and by psychic influence, the term astral often denotes a negative context.

4. Mark 10: 14–15.

5. Cayce, *Dreams,* reading 294-56, pp. 47–48. We see that in this dream practical advice is given, which when followed, as we presume Edgar Cayce did, could bring restoration of normal brain functioning.

6. Elsie Sechrist, *Dreams: Your Magic Mirror* (Virginia Beach, Va.: A.R.E. Press, 1995), pp. 69–70.

7. Ibid., p. 73.

8. I Sam. 3:1–10.

9. Ann Spangler, *Dreams: True Stories of Remarkable Encounters with God* (Grand Rapids, Mich.: Zondervan Publishing House, 1997), p. 30.

10. Ibid., p. 29.

Chapter Six: *Creating Your Dream Journal*

1. Edgar Cayce, *A.R.E. Journal No. 6* (Virginia Beach, Va.: A.R.E. Press, 1972), p. 279.

2. Gayle Delaney, Ph.D., *All about Dreams: Everything You Need to Know about Why We Have Them, What They Mean, and How to Put Them to Work for You* (HarperSanFrancisco, 1998), pp. 269–70.

3. As promised, here are some dream dictionaries that you may find helpful: See James R. Lewis, *The Dream Encyclopedia* (Detroit, Mich.: Visible Ink Press, 1995); Alice Anne Parker, *Understand Your Dreams: 1,001 Basic Dream Images and How to Interpret Them* (Tiburon, Calif.: H. J. Kramer, 1991); Lady Stearn Robinson and Tom Corbett, *The Dreamer's Dictionary: From A to Z...3,000 Magical Mirrors to Reveal the Meaning of Your Dreams* (New York: Warner Books, 1974); Klaus Vollmar, *The Little Giant Encyclopedia of Dream Symbols* (New York: Sterling Publishing Co., 1997). I particularly like *The Dream Encyclopedia* because it has very useful information about dreams in addition to a dictionary of symbols.

Chapter Seven: *Discoveries from the Land of Shadows*

1. For more information on the shadow, see page 228 note 1. On the anima and animus, see page 228 note 2.

2. The violet flame is an aspect of the Holy Spirit that can be invoked by prayer, decrees or affirmations. It is a spiritual fire, a frequency of spiritual energy that transmutes (transforms) negative attitudes, thoughts, feelings and habit patterns into positive potential. To learn more, see the following Summit University Press publications by Elizabeth Clare Prophet: *Violet Flame to Heal Body, Mind and Soul,* pocket guide; *Spiritual Techniques to Heal Body, Mind and Soul,* 90-minute audiocassette album.

3. See the nondenominational rosaries *A Child's Rosary to Mother Mary,* for adults and children. These 15-minute scriptural rosaries are a universal prayer that can be given by people of all faiths. Scriptural readings are from the New Testament. Available on audiocassette and CD, published by Summit University Press.

4. See Larry Dossey, M.D., *Prayer Is Good Medicine* (New York: HarperCollins, 1996). Norman Vincent Peale, *The Power of Positive Thinking* (Englewood Cliffs, N.J.: Prentice-Hall, 1952). Paul Pearsall, Ph.D., *The Heart's Code: Tapping the Wisdom and Power of Our Heart Energy* (New York: Bantam Doubleday Dell Publishing Group, Broadway Books, 1998). Martin L. Rossman, M.D., *Healing Yourself: A Step-by-Step Program for Better Health through Imagery* (New York: Pocket Books, 1987).

5. See Sara Paddison, *The Hidden Power of the Heart: Achieving Balance and Fulfillment in a Stressful World* (Boulder Creek, Calif.: Planetary Publications, 1995).

6. See Mark L. Prophet and Elizabeth Clare Prophet, *The Science of the Spoken Word* (Corwin Springs, Mont.: 1991), p. 72.

7. Esoterically, the aura is the rainbow-colored energy field surrounding the soul and the etheric, mental, emotional and physical "bodies" or energy sheaths that are the modes of the soul's journey in time and space. The aura is also referred to as the "L" field, which some scientists say controls the manifestation of the physical body. For further information, see *The Human Aura: How to Activate and Energize Your Aura and Chakras,* by Kuthumi and Djwal Kul (Corwin Springs, Mont.: Summit University Press, 1996).

8. See Mark L. Prophet and Elizabeth Clare Prophet, *The Science of the Spoken Word,* p. 114.

9. Ibid., p. 113.

Chapter Eight: *Dreams as Messages from Higher Realms*

1. Michel de Montaigne, "Of Experience," *Essays* (1588), trans. Charles Cotton and W. C. Hazlitt.

2. See Elizabeth Clare Prophet, "Teachings on the Path of the Ruby Ray," Feb. 14, 1998.

3. See Annice Booth, *Memories of Mark: My Life with Mark Prophet* (Corwin Springs, Mont.: Summit University Press, 1999).

Chapter Nine: *Etheric Studies in the Heaven World*

1. In the Jewish mystical tradition of the Kabbalah, the sefirot are the ten aspects of God's being that manifested from the Infinite (Ein Sof). Kabbalists' diagram of the sefirot, called the Tree of Life, is a blueprint for divine and human action and interaction. For a profound and lucid understanding of the mystical concepts of the Kabbalah, see Elizabeth Clare Prophet with Patricia R. Spadaro and Murray L. Steinman, *Kabbalah: Key to Your Inner Power* (Corwin Springs, Mont.: Summit University Press, 1997).

2. See Annice Booth, *The Path to Your Ascension: Rediscovering Life's Ultimate Purpose* (1999) and Serapis Bey, *Dossier on the Ascension: The Story of the Soul's Acceleration into Higher Consciousness on the Path of Initiation* (1978), published by Summit University Press.

3. Kuan Yin of fearlessness and Kuan Yin of moon and water are two of the thirty-three manifestations of Kuan Yin, which have been venerated in China since the seventh century. The mantras to the thirty-three manifestations are included on *Kuan Yin's Crystal Rosary: Devotions to the Divine Mother East and West,* a New Age ritual of hymns, prayers and Chinese mantras that invokes the merciful presence of Kuan Yin, Bodhisattva of Compassion. Available on 3-audiocassette album and on CD, released by Elizabeth Clare Prophet, published by Summit University Press.

4. Babaji is an *avatara,* a title in Hindu scriptures signifying the descent of Divinity into flesh. Paramahansa Yogananda revealed this timeless master's existence to the public in 1946. He revered

Babaji as a *Mahavatar* (Great Avatar) and Yogi-Christ of modern India. He said Babaji is ever in communion with Christ, and his mission in India is to assist prophets in carrying out their special dispensations. For a fascinating description of Babaji's miracles and enduring service to the people of Earth, see chapters 33 and 34 of Yogananda's book *Autobiography of a Yogi* (1946; reprint, Los Angeles: Self-Realization Fellowship, 1974).

5. Yogananda explains *samadhi* as a blissful superconscious state in which the yogi experiences his identity as both individualized soul and Cosmic Spirit. Yogananda differentiates between the two states of samadhi. *Sabikalpa samadhi* is a state of bliss in which the devotee attains realization of oneness with Spirit but can only maintain his cosmic consciousness in an immobile trance state. *Nirbikalpa samadhi* is the attainment of immutable bliss and realization where the devotee realizes fully his identity with Spirit and moves freely in the world without any loss of God-perception. See Yogananda, *Autobiography of a Yogi,* pp. 9, 126, 275–86, 477.

6. The Dark Night of the Spirit is an advanced initiation of the soul striving for union with God. Elizabeth Clare Prophet has taught that in this advanced initiation the awareness of the presence of God, given by grace, is suspended and the soul must experience reunion with God through the soul's own attainment. This is the experience that Master Jesus had on the cross when he momentarily felt a separation from God and cried out, "Eli, Eli, lama sabachthani?" that is to say, "My God, my God, why hast thou forsaken me?" (Matt. 27:46).

7. Dannion Brinkley with Paul Perry, *Saved by the Light* (New York: Villard Books, 1994). Betty J. Eadie, *Embraced by the Light* (Placerville, Calif.: Gold Leaf Press, 1992). George G. Ritchie with Elizabeth Sherrill, *Return from Tomorrow* (Grand Rapids, Mich.: Fleming H. Revell, 1978).

8. Melvin Morse, M.D., with Paul Perry, *Closer to the Light: Learning from the Near-Death Experiences of Children* (New York: Ballantine Books, Ivy Books, 1991), p. 167.

9. From the teachings of Mark and Elizabeth Prophet. For more information on the threefold flame, see the Prophets' book *The Lost Teachings of Jesus 2,* pocketbook ed. (Corwin Springs, Mont.: Summit University), pp. 82–86.

10. Tanner, *The Mystical, Magical, Marvelous World of Dreams,* p. 23.

11. Luke 9:28–32.

12. *Kuthumi on Selfhood: Consciousness: The Doorway to Reality* (Corwin Springs, Mont.: Summit University Press, 1979), p. 170; also published as a *Pearl of Wisdom,* vol. 12, no. 39.

Chapter Ten: *Lucid Dreaming and Tibetan Yoga*

1. Reported in Jayne Gackenbach and Jane Bosveld, *Control Your Dreams* (New York: Harper and Row, 1989).

2. Interview with Tenzin Wangyal Rinpoche, in *Snow Lion,* summer 1998 newsletter and catalog supplement (vol. 13, no. 3) p. 1.

3. The Four Noble Truths of the Buddha are (1) life is pain (suffering); (2) pain arises from cravings (inordinate desires); (3) cessation of pain comes through forsaking or nonattachment to cravings; and (4) the way of nonattachment is the Noble Eightfold Way (Path), namely, right views (understanding), right intention, right speech, right action, right livelihood, right effort, right mindfulness, right contemplation.

4. Tenzin Wangyal Rinpoche, *The Tibetan Yogas of Dream and Sleep* (Ithaca, N.Y.: Snow Lion Publications, 1998), p. 93.

5. Interview with Rinpoche, *Snow Lion,* p. 2.

6. For the Tibetan way of doing this practice, see Rinpoche, *The Tibetan Yogas of Dream and Sleep,* pp. 104–18. The terms "wrathful deities" and "wrathful and vengeful deities" originate in the ancient text of *The Tibetan Book of the Dead* as characteristics of the "First Bardo."

7. Interview with Rinpoche, *Snow Lion,* p. 2.

8. Carla McAuley, "Aubrey Said...," 1996.

9. Rinpoche, *The Tibetan Yogas of Dream and Sleep,* p. 149.

10. Interview with Rinpoche, *Snow Lion,* p. 3.

Chapter Eleven: *Dream Analysis from the Adept's Point of View*

1. John 2:1–11.

2. C. W. Leadbeater, *Dreams: What They Are and How They Are Caused* (1903; reprint, Kila, Mont.: Kessinger Publishing), p. 24.

The additional material on Leadbeater's view of dream analysis is a summary of pages 24–36, 49–50.

3. Ibid., p. 34.

4. Ibid., p. 36.

5. Eph. 4:26.

6. Leadbeater, *Dreams,* pp. 68–69.

7. Elizabeth Clare Prophet, "Lecture on Soul Mates," *Twin Flames in Love,* July 5, 1982.

8. Elizabeth Clare Prophet, "Lecture on John the Beloved," Summit University, Nov. 17, 1982.

9. Elizabeth Clare Prophet, "Climb the Highest Mountain," Summit University, Oct. 8, 1973.

10. Elizabeth Clare Prophet, "On Dealing with Death, Discarnates and Malevolent Spirits, Part 2," Feb. 18, 1991.

11. Mark L. Prophet, "The Lure of the Wild—A Study in Obsession, Cause and Cure: Exorcism and Restoration," *Pyramid Conference,* Oct. 10, 1969.

12. Elizabeth Clare Prophet, *The Lost Years of Jesus,* pocketbook ed. (Corwin Springs, Mont.: Summit University Press, 1987), pp. 272–73.

13. Nicholas Roerich, "Dreams," in *Shambhala: In Search of the New Era* (Rochester, Vt.: Inner Traditions International, 1990), pp. 130–32.

14. El Morya, devotee of the will of God, was embodied as the Master M., one of the founders of the Theosophical Society in the late 1800s. He was also embodied as Akbar, greatest of the Mogul emperors, described by a noted historian as "one of the few successful examples of Plato's philosopher-king." For a rich history of the past lives and works of this magnificent ascended master, see Mark L. Prophet and Elizabeth Clare Prophet's *Lords of the Seven Rays* (Corwin Springs, Mont.: Summit University Press, 1986), book 1, chapter 1.

15. The Great White Brotherhood is a spiritual order of Western saints and Eastern adepts who have transcended the cycles of karma and rebirth and ascended into the heaven world. They are known as ascended masters. The Brotherhood also includes the

archangels and other advanced spiritual beings as well as some unascended beings. The "white" in the name denotes the aura of white light, the halo that surrounds these spiritual beings.

16. Elizabeth Clare Prophet, "Reading from Nicholas Roerich's *Shambhala*," Summit University, Nov. 5, 1981.

Chapter Twelve: *Nicholas Roerich's Dreams: A Message for Our Soul*

1. Rom. 7:19.

2. For further understanding of the spiritual initiations of the Dark Night of the Soul, see Mark L. Prophet and Elizabeth Clare Prophet, *The Lost Teachings of Jesus 4* (Corwin Springs, Mont.: Summit University Press, 1993), chapter 13.

3. For the story of Siddhartha, see *Quietly Comes the Buddha: Awakening Your Inner Buddha-Nature,* by Elizabeth Clare Prophet with introduction by Karen Y. LeBeau (Corwin Springs, Mont.: Summit University Press, 1998).

4. I Cor. 13:12–13.

5. For a thorough understanding of Kabbalistic concepts, see Elizabeth Clare Prophet, *Kabbalah: Key to Your Inner Power.*

6. For a down-to-earth understanding of the path to our ultimate reunion with our God through the initiation of the ascension, see Booth, *The Path to Your Ascension.*

7. Serapis Bey, in 1967 *Pearls of Wisdom,* vol. 10, no. 18, published by Summit University Press.

Bibliography

Abdalati, Hammudah. *Islam in Focus.* Islamic Book Service, 1996.

Agni Yoga Society. *Heart.* New York: Agni Yoga Society, 1975.

Babylonian Talmud, trans. Michael L. Rodkinson. 2nd ed. New York: New Talmud Publishing Co., 1901.

Barrick, Marilyn C. *Sacred Psychology of Love: The Quest for Relationships That Unite Heart and Soul.* Corwin Springs, Mont.: Summit University Press, 1999.

Bonime, Walter. *The Clinical Use of Dreams.* New York: Basic Books, 1962.

Booth, Annice. *Memories of Mark: My Life with Mark Prophet.* Corwin Springs, Mont.: Summit University Press, 1999.

Booth, Annice. *The Path to Your Ascension.* Corwin Springs, Mont.: Summit University Press, 1999.

Brinkley, Dannion with Paul Perry. *Saved by the Light.* New York: Villard Books, 1994.

Brown, Tom, Jr. *Grandfather.* New York: Berkley Publishing Group, Berkley Books, 1993.

Cayce, Hugh Lynn, et al. *Dreams: The Language of the Unconscious.* Virginia Beach, Va.: A.R.E. Press, 1971.

Corsini, Raymond J., and Alan J. Auerbach. *Concise Encyclopedia of Psychology.* 2nd ed., abr. New York: John Wiley & Sons, 1998.

Cunningham, Scott. *Dreaming the Divine: Techniques for Sacred Sleep.* St. Paul, Minn.: Llewellyn Publications, 1999.

Delaney, Gayle, Ph.D. *All about Dreams: Everything You Need to Know about Why We Have Them, What They Mean, and How to Put Them to Work for You.* HarperSanFrancisco, 1998.

Delaney, Gayle, Ph.D. *Living Your Dreams.* New York: HarperCollins Publishers, 1996.

Dement, William, M.D. *Some Must Watch While Some Must Sleep.* San Francisco: San Francisco Book Co., 1976.

Dossey, Larry, M.D. *Prayer Is Good Medicine.* New York: Harper-Collins, 1996.

Eadie, Betty J. *Embraced by the Light.* Placerville, Calif.: Gold Leaf Press, 1992.

Ferrucci, Piero. *What We May Be: Techniques for Psychological and Spiritual Growth.* Los Angeles: J. P. Tarcher, 1982.

Fontana, David. *Understanding and Using Your Dreams.* Great Britain: Element Books Limited, 1990.

Gackenbach, Jayne, and Jane Bosveld. *Control Your Dreams.* New York: Harper and Row, 1989.

Hall, Manley P. *The Secret Teachings of All Ages.* Los Angeles: The Philosophical Research Society, 1977.

Hill, Clara E. *Working with Dreams in Psychotherapy.* New York: Guilford Press, 1996.

Holy Bible: Scofield Reference Edition.

Homer, *Illiad.*

Homer, *Odyssey.*

Jung, Carl G., et al. *Man and His Symbols.* Garden City, N.Y.: Doubleday & Company, 1964.

Kelsey, Morton T. *God, Dreams, and Revelation: A Christian Interpretation of Dreams.* Rev. ed. Minneapolis, Minn.: Augsburg Fortress, 1991.

Kramer, Samuel Noah. *The Sumerians: Their History, Culture, and Character.* Chicago: University of Chicago Press, 1963.

Kuthumi on Selfhood: Consciousness: The Doorway to Reality. Corwin Springs, Mont.: Summit University Press, 1969.

Kuthumi, and Djwal Kul. *The Human Aura: How to Activate and Energize Your Aura and Chakras.* Corwin Springs, Mont.: Summit University Press, 1982.

Lawrence, Lauren. *Dream Keys: Unlocking the Power of Your Unconscious Mind.* New York: Dell Publishing, 1999.

Leadbeater, C. W. *Dreams: What They Are and How They Are Caused.* 1903. Reprint. Kila, Mont.: Kessinger Publishing.

Leadbeater, Charles W. *The Inner Life.* Wheaton, Ill.: Theosophical Publishing House, 1978.

Lewis, James R. *The Dream Encyclopedia.* Detroit, Mich.: Visible Ink Press, 1995.

Mazza, Joan. *Dreaming Your Real Self: A Personal Approach to Dream Interpretation.* New York: Perigee Book, 1998.

Millman, Dan. *Way of the Peaceful Warrior: A Book That Changes Lives.* Tiburon, Calif.: H. J. Kramer, 1984.

Moore, Thomas. *Care of the Soul: A Guide for Cultivating Depth and Sacredness in Everyday Life.* New York: HarperCollins, 1992.

Morse, Melvin, M.D., with Paul Perry. *Closer to the Light: Learning from the Near-Death Experiences of Children.* New York: Ballantine Books, Ivy Books, 1991.

Paddison, Sara. *The Hidden Power of the Heart: Achieving Balance and Fulfillment in a Stressful World.* Boulder Creek, Calif.: Planetary Publications, 1995.

Parker, Alice Anne. *Understand Your Dreams: 1,001 Basic Dream Images and How to Interpret Them.* Tiburon, Calif.: H. J. Kramer, 1991.

Peale, Norman Vincent. *The Power of Positive Thinking.* Englewood Cliffs, N.J.: Prentice-Hall, 1952.

Pearsall, Paul, Ph.D. *The Heart's Code: Tapping the Wisdom and Power of Our Heart Energy.* New York: Bantam Doubleday Dell Publishing Group, 1998.

Peers, E. Allison, trans. and ed. *The Complete Works of Saint John of the Cross.* Dark Night of the Soul, vol. 1. Westminster, Md.: Newman Press, 1953.

Prophet, Elizabeth Clare. "Climb the Highest Mountain." Summit University, Oct. 8, 1973.

Prophet, Elizabeth Clare. "Lecture on John the Beloved." Summit University, Nov. 17, 1982.

Prophet, Elizabeth Clare. "Lecture on Soul Mates." *Twin Flames in Love* conference, July 5, 1982.

Prophet, Elizabeth Clare. *The Lost Years of Jesus.* Corwin Springs, Mont.: Summit University Press, 1984.

Prophet, Elizabeth Clare. "On Dealing with Death, Discarnates and

Malevolent Spirits, Part 2." Lecture tour, Feb. 18, 1991.

Prophet, Elizabeth Clare. *Violet Flame to Heal Body, Mind and Soul.* Corwin Springs, Mont.: Summit University Press, 1997.

Prophet, Elizabeth Clare, with introduction by Karen Y. LeBeau. *Quietly Comes the Buddha: Awakening Your Inner Buddha-Nature.* Corwin Springs, Mont.: Summit University Press, 1998.

Prophet, Elizabeth Clare, with Patricia R. Spadaro. *The Art of Practical Spirituality: How to Bring More Passion, Creativity and Balance into Everyday Life.* Corwin Springs, Mont.: Summit University Press, 2000.

Prophet, Elizabeth Clare, with Patricia R. Spadaro and Murray L. Steinman. *Kabbalah: Key to Your Inner Power.* Corwin Springs, Mont.: Summit University Press, 1997.

Prophet, Mark L. "The Lure of the Wild—A Study in Obsession, Cause and Core: Exorcism and Restoration." *Pyramid Conference,* Oct. 10, 1969.

Prophet, Mark L., and Elizabeth Clare Prophet. *Lords of the Seven Rays: Mirror of Consciousness.* Corwin Springs, Mont.: Summit University Press, 1986.

Prophet, Mark L., and Elizabeth Clare Prophet. *The Lost Teachings of Jesus 1–4,* pocketbook ed. Corwin Springs, Mont.: Summit University Press, 1993–1994.

Prophet, Mark L., and Elizabeth Clare Prophet. *The Science of the Spoken Word.* Corwin Springs, Mont.: Summit University Press, 1983.

Reid, Clyde H. *Dreams: Discovering Your Inner Teacher.* Minneapolis, Minn.: Winston Press, 1983.

Rinpoche, Tenzin Wangyal. *The Tibetan Yogas of Dream and Sleep.* Ithaca, N.Y.: Snow Lion Publications, 1998.

Ritchie, George G., with Elizabeth Sherrill. *Return from Tomorrow.* Grand Rapids, Mich.: Baker Book House, 1978.

Robinson, Lady Stearn, and Tom Corbett. *The Dreamer's Dictionary: From A to Z...3,000 Magical Mirrors to Reveal the Meaning of Your Dreams.* New York: Warner Books, 1994.

Roerich, Nicholas. *Shambhala: In Search of the New Era.* Rochester, Vt.: Inner Traditions International, 1990.

Rossman, Martin L., M.D. *Healing Yourself: A Step-by-Step Program for Better Health through Imagery.* New York: Pocket Books, 1987.

Saint Germain On Alchemy: For the Adept in the Aquarian Age. Corwin Springs, Mont.: Summit University Press, 1985.

Sechrist, Elsie. *Dreams: Your Magic Mirror.* Virginia Beach, Va.: A.R.E. Press, 1995.

Serapis Bey. *Dossier on the Ascension: The Story of the Soul's Acceleration into Higher Consciousness on the Path of Initiation.* Corwin Springs, Mont.: Summit University Press, 1979.

Serapis Bey. 1967 *Pearls of Wisdom.* Corwin Springs, Mont.: Summit University Press, 1967.

Snow, Chet B., Ph.D. *Mass Dreams of the Future,* featuring Hypnotic Future-Life Progressions by Helen Wambach, Ph.D. New York: McGraw-Hill Publishing Company, 1989.

Snow Lion. Snow Lion Publications. www.snowlionpub.com

Soymié, Michel. *Les songes et leur interprétations: Sources orientales.* Paris: Seuil, 1959.

Spangler, Ann. *Dreams: True Stories of Remarkable Encounters with God.* Grand Rapids, Mich.: ZondervanPublishingHouse, 1997.

Tanner, Wilda B. *The Mystical, Magical, Marvelous World of Dreams.* Tahlequah, Okla.: Sparrow Hawk Press, 1988.

Tibetan Book of the Dead, trans. Robert A. F. Thurman. New York: Quality Paperback Book Club, 1998.

Vollmar, Klaus. *The Little Giant Encyclopedia of Dream Symbols.* New York: Sterling Publishing Co., 1997.

Woods, Ralph L., ed. *The World of Dreams.* New York: Random House, 1947.

Yogananda, Paramahansa. *Autobiography of a Yogi.* 1946. Reprint. Los Angeles: Self-Realization Fellowship, 1974.

Zweig, Connie, Ph.D., and Steve Wolf, Ph.D. *Romancing the Shadow: Illuminating the Dark Side of the Soul.* New York: Ballantine Books, 1997.

Marilyn C. Barrick, Ph.D., is a clinical psychologist, minister and author of two popular books, *Sacred Psychology of Love: The Quest for Relationships That Unite Heart and Soul* and *Sacred Psychology of Change: Life as a Voyage of Transformation.*

Combining psychological expertise and in-depth spiritual understanding, Dr. Barrick specializes in spiritual psychology and transformational work, dream analysis, inner-child work, relationship counseling, Gestalt techniques, spiritual self-help exercises and EMDR trauma-release therapy. In addition to her private practice, she conducts workshops in the U.S.A., Canada and Europe.

Dr. Barrick has consulted as a psychological expert to schools, government agencies, professional advisory boards and mental health facilities. In the 1960s and early 1970s, she taught graduate courses for the Department of Psychology at the University of Colorado and served with the Peace Corps as a training development officer and field counselor. Since 1976, she has been a minister in a church that integrates the spiritual teachings of the world's major religions.

Dr. Barrick's perspective on dreams and her intriguing examples of dream analysis in her book *Dreams: Exploring the Secrets of Your Soul* are drawn from her clinical practice and ministry. As she puts it, "Dreams are a window through which we view the secrets of our soul. And dream analysis becomes a sacred adventure, where we explore the very essence of who we are and who we may become."

Visit Dr. Barrick's web site at www.spiritualpsychology.com.

Are emotional blocks holding you back?

*Heal your soul with the Sacred Psychology series
and claim the abundance and mastery
that are yours!*

ISBN: 0-922729-77-8
Trade Paperback $14.95

EMOTIONS

Transforming Anger, Fear and Pain

BY MARILYN C. BARRICK, PH.D.

Scientists have demonstrated the link between emotional balance and physical and mental well-being. In this work, Dr. Marilyn Barrick takes the study of our emotions—and how to deal with them—to the next level. She offers psychological expertise and in-depth spiritual understanding to guide us through our emotional ups and downs, showing us how to release anger, guilt and grief in a healthy way to experience inner joy. An invaluable guide to creating heart-centeredness in a turbulent world.

"Marilyn Barrick is on the mark. While we search for the understanding of our physical, mental and spiritual selves, we often forget the source of the balance between all of them—our emotional self. This book addresses the issue magnificently. Read it and grow."

—DANNION BRINKLEY,
N.Y. Times bestselling author of
Saved by the Light and *At Peace in the Light*

*"*Emotions *is a wise, heartfelt and deeply spiritual path that can lead you from fear to courage, anger to joy, and helplessness to effectiveness —whatever challenges you may be facing. I have found it tremendously helpful."*

—MARTIN L. ROSSMAN, M.D.
author of *Guided Imagery for Self-Healing*

SACRED PSYCHOLOGY OF LOVE

*The Quest for Relationships
That Unite Heart and Soul*

BY MARILYN C. BARRICK, PH.D.

Unfolds the hidden spiritual and psychological dramas inherent in friendships, love relationships and marriage.

*"A wonderful marriage of the mystical
and practical, this soul-nourishing book
is beautiful, healing and thought-provoking."*

—SUE PATTON THOELE,
author, *Heart Centered Marriage*

ISBN: 0-922729-49-2
Trade Paperback $12.95

SACRED PSYCHOLOGY OF CHANGE

Life as a Voyage of Transformation
BY MARILYN C. BARRICK, PH.D.

Shows how you can welcome cycles of change and even chaos as transformational opportunities. Discover the importance of a creative mind-set, an open heart and the maturing of soul to meet the challenges of endings, beginnings and waves of change.

"This book will lead you, chapter by chapter and step by step, to a profoundly healing dialogue with yourself—and through an exciting spiritual and psychological journey of change."

—KENNETH FRAZIER,
L.P.C., D.A.P.A., A.C.P.E.

ISBN: 0-922729-57-3
Trade Paperback $14.95

FOR MORE INFORMATION

Summit University Press books are available at fine
bookstores worldwide and at your favorite on-line book-
seller. Our books have been translated into 20 languages
and are sold in more than 30 markets worldwide.

For a free catalog of Summit University Press books
and products or to learn more about the spiritual techniques featured in this book, please contact:

Summit University Press
PO Box 5000
Corwin Springs, MT 59030-5000 USA
Telephone: 1-800-245-5445 or 406-848-9500
Fax: 1-800-221-8307 or 406-848-9555
E-mail:info@summituniversitypress.com
www.summituniversitypress.com